PRAISE FOR *THE SECRETS OF COLD CALL SUCCESS*

"If you are one of those people who think cold calling is dead, then you haven't met Paul M. Neuberger. In his book, *The Secrets to Cold Call Success,* Paul shares the essential five building blocks and a comprehensive step-by-step guide to help improve your effectiveness for this still very import-ant tool in your sales toolbox. Simply put…his strategies and techniques work even in our current social media/digitally focused business environment. Pick up a copy for you and the rest of your sales team before your competitors do!"

—*Wayne Breitbarth*
Author of the bestselling book The Power
Formula for LinkedIn Success: Kick-start Your
Business Brand, *and* Job Search

"Give something, not get something. Give the prospect something without expecting to get something back. Sounds like a simple concept doesn't it? It is, and it works! The simplicity is what makes it brilliant. And the way it works, supported by human nature, makes it fool proof.

Paul's methods work. I've done it, our people at Zebrafi have done it, and our customers have done it. He trans-formed the toughest part of our go-to-market; getting peo-ple to start a conversation with us. Our productivity is up 300%! We have two points in time at Zebrafi, BP and AP: Before Paul and After Paul. That is how profound the differ-ence is! I endorse Paul because I know him personally, have watched him and others work his process, and succeed!"

—*Jeff Koser*
Founder & CEO of Zebrafi, Inc.
Award-Winning author of Selling to Zebras

"To schedule more meetings faster, study, digest and practice what you read in this book."

Author of Eat Their Lunch: Winning Customers
Away from Your Competition

"I just wanted to take a quick moment to personally thank you for changing the way we call prospects. The approach is logical and fun and I certainly have more confidence when cold calling. As someone who built a multi-million-dollar book of business on cold calling the 'wrong' way I am very thankful we started working together. All I can say is where were you 20 years ago?! Thanks again and I look forward to continuing to build on what we started."

—*Greg Prentice*
CEO & Senior Advisor / Reseco Insurance Advisors, LLC

"To say Paul's training has been transformative for me personally and my team is an understatement. His comprehensive approach teaches not only the components of an effective call but the psychology behind these connections. He has driven focus on our message and core purpose with every call and client interaction."

—*Margaret Dallmann*
Vice President of Sales / Health Payment Systems

"Paul's framework for successfully scripting calls gives cold callers a new level of confidence when they are reaching out to potential customers and helps them sound like a normal person rather than the stereotypical 'smarmy salesperson.' This framework has also helped me personally to know who I should be reaching out to, what to say when I do, and how to get callbacks when I don't connect. I'd highly recommend Paul to anyone who is looking to increase their knowledge, be more effective on the phone, and ultimately advance their sales career."

—*Cody Garvin*
Sales Manager / Express Employment Professionals

"Paul's philosophy is a complete departure from typical cold call training! After going through the training and booking several one-on-one sessions, Paul's approach has radically changed my appointment-setting results."

—*David Cantliffe*
President & Founder / BottomLine Advantage, LLC

"This is just what I needed and when I needed it! Mr. Neuberger's professional and engaging delivery and his personal, caring approach to his vocation suits me and my learning style."

—*Chillon Leach*
Textile Artist / Self-Employed

"Your training has been extremely helpful and has certainly lifted my spirits a bit as I haven't had a single person hang up on me since I started your approach. Additionally, my numbers are all quite a bit higher. Thanks so much for your help, it's been well worth the investment."

—*Brian Fellers*
Market Manager / Best Version Media

"I am very thankful for your insight. I am getting an appointment 85% of the time! The other 15% are at least responding to my contact. Paul, I am really getting results and enjoying it! I review your program and techniques often. It has made the biggest impact for me and I am finding many opportunities. Your desire to make a difference is helping me also make a difference."

—*Jeanne Koshick*
Business Development & Clinical Specialist / NXC Imaging

"Brilliant, yet simple. You'll wonder why you didn't see it all along. Paul is an engaging educator, so much so that he takes the dread out of cold calling and makes it easy, effective and doable, for everyone. Highly, highly recommend his system."

—*Linda Layber*
District Sales Coordinator / Aflac

"The expression 'Cold Calling is Dead' could not be more far from the truth—people have simply been convinced that it no longer works based upon their experience and ultimate failures when it is not used properly. Paul's approach and expertise in helping you script your cold call message is spot on. His method will yield results that can be measurable for your business if you let him re-teach you everything you have learned about picking up the phone and calling a cold contact. Paul takes you through a process that requires thought and relentless pursuit of perfecting your message which results in a laser focused, quality first impression cold call. Voicemail? Paul has an answer for that as well. Cannot get past the 'pit bull' answering the phone? Paul has an answer for that. Thank you, Paul. You have transformed my business with your tutelage."

—*Tom Feldhusen*
Executive Adviser / Culture Index

"I have been selling for 37 years and The Cold Call Coach is the first person I have 100% bought into. Paul has an engaging personality combined with a passionate delivery and most importantly I feel that Paul is truly interested in my success. With past sales trainers, I have only felt they were after my money. I whole heartedly recommend Paul's sales program to anyone anywhere on the selling continuum."

—*Ed Winiarski*
Account Executive / Arjo

"I haven't seen anything like The Cold Call Coach during my 27 years in the sales industry. Paul has the best training for anyone or company that depends on the phone call to create income. Before stepping into Paul's training, I would have told anyone that I am a very good salesperson on the phone. I thought a good cold call success rate was around 26%. To my amazement, after one week of access to Paul's career-changing material, I accumulated an 89% cold call success rate. Come on, an 89% cold call rate?! That's the kind of stuff that changes lives. It sure changed mine! I have maintained a cold call success rate at that level as of today. Thanks to Paul I have a clear plan for every cold call. Paul's training is great for any industry, but, I must say, it is amazing in mine!"

—*Wayne Glenn*
Sales Manager / Russ Darrow Group

"Just wanted to thank you. I am seven weeks into this position after 15 years in retail. Cold calling is the only thing I have struggled with and after your seminar, I have a new confidence and feel I have my own approach."

—*Samantha Lang*
Business Development Manager / Accounting Principals

"Let me just say your training is amazing! During my 15 years in the financial industry (over a few companies and positions) I have never seen or heard of such an effective strategy to calling and getting appointments without sounding 'salesy.' I wish I would have known this a long time ago! Needless to say, I truly value what you have taught us."

—*Adam Fullmer*
Branch Manager / UW Credit Union

"I would highly recommend Paul's training to companies and individuals who are looking to build their sales. My sales team has gained more confidence in their cold calling and Paul has given us a game plan that works and that we are excited to use. The techniques he shared are innovative and in the short time since we have implemented them, all members of my team are experiencing success."

—*Lauren Herlache*
Sales Manager / Signarama

"Since my first few sessions with Paul Neuberger, I have seen my cold call success rate jump from 5%–10% up to nearly 75%. If I was short on time and only had a moment to write down one piece to illustrate my cold call success, that would be the proverbial 'dagger.' As it so happens, I find myself with a bit of free time to say that Paul really has made a difference in my business. I have gotten in front of individuals who, without the Cold Call Coach, I would have been too hesitant to call. My piece of advice...do yourself a favor...don't be too hesitant to give Paul a call."

—*Colin Schreck*
Loan Officer / Bank of England Mortgage

"I used to make about 200 calls to book an appointment and very few voicemails got returned. Now about 50% of my conversations become appointments and about 20% of my voicemails get returned. That's life changing—and I couldn't be happier."

—*Matthew Gillard*
Account Executive / McLean Hallmark Insurance Group

PAUL M. NEUBERGER

THE SECRETS
TO COLD CALL SUCCESS

Close More Business in
Less Time Than Ever Before

Cover design by Jessika Savage

Book design by Alex Head / Draft Lab

ISBN: 978-1-7350396-0-2

Printed in the United States of America

DEDICATION

*I dedicate this book to the two most
important people in my life.*

*The first is God, who sent His only begotten Son,
Jesus Christ, to die for my sins so that I may have
Eternal Life. This incomprehensible act of love inspires
me to be the best version of myself every day.*

*The second is my wife and best friend, Tanya,
the glue that holds our family together. Without her
unwavering support of and trust in me, none of this
would be possible. I love you, Tanny Bear.*

TABLE OF CONTENTS

PREFACE

One morning, my father-in-law got up early, like he usually did, went into the living room and sat on the couch. He then bent down to put on his socks and never came back up. He had a fatal heart attack, and just like that he was gone. He died on November 2, 2012, which also happened to be his 60th birthday.

Losing someone you love, especially unexpectedly, is extremely difficult. He always wanted grandkids, and my wife, Tanya, and I were able to bring that joy into his life—albeit briefly. He passed less than two months after our first child, Kennedy, was born.

My father-in-law didn't have life insurance. As an independent contractor, he didn't have a large corporate retirement account. So when he died, it became apparent my mother-in-law's financial situation would be more difficult than it had to be. On top of her grief, she faced a challenging financial future and it didn't have to be that way. I blamed myself. Why didn't I see this brewing years before? Could I have prevented it? How did I let this happen to people I love?

It dawned on me that my family's situation was not unique. Millions face unexpected financial hardships that could be prevented or significantly decreased with proactive planning. I decided to leave the world of college administration to become a financial advisor, with the goal of helping people avoid the situation my family was now enduring.

I loved my new job at Thrivent Financial, but it was the first position where I didn't receive a guaranteed salary. My compensation was now a hundred percent commission. And I'd be lying if I said I wasn't at least a little bit scared of making this career move. In my previous role, I was cold calling against the backdrop of a steady, regular paycheck, but now I would be cold calling without that safety net. My livelihood and ability to provide for my family depended on mastering this skill.

I don't want to disparage my former employer, but the scripts they gave me left a lot to be desired. I read through them and thought, this is never going to work! I'm never going to get an appointment if I use these scripts! This is a surefire way to guarantee that my family goes hungry, so I might as well give up now!

But that's not me. I'm a tenacious SOB, so I made a decision to come up with a better way. How could I improve this from start to finish? Could I create a once-for-all-time, world-class cold call script? How could I differentiate myself and present a better value proposition than my competitors?

I was not an overnight sensation. But over the course of several months, I developed a unique approach that was astonishingly effective. Over time, using my method, I could make 15 cold calls and schedule 15 appointments. Everybody and their mother wanted to know how I was doing it, and I started gaining a reputation as a cold calling virtuoso—both inside and outside my company. People started asking if they could pay me to train their sales-people, write scripts for them, heck, even sit in my office and listen to me cold call my prospects. It was all happening so fast!

This was the birth of The Cold Call Coach, a business I started to help people master the art and science behind cold calling once and for all. After a few months, my side business became my full-time vocation in order to meet the insatiable demand for my services.

Since then, I've brought my proprietary methodology to individuals in more than 120 countries and partnered with leading organizations across the U.S. I will share with you many of their stories. Though some of the names have been changed to protect the privacy of former clients, their experiences and results have not.

The secret to my success is I can get in front of who I want, when I want, for whatever reason I want.

How do I do it?

In this book I will teach you.

INTRODUCTION

What if you could connect with anyone, whenever you wanted, and actually have them listen to what you have to say? What doors would that open for you? Who would you want to meet? How could it impact your career?

Perhaps you'd meet with the executives making massive purchasing decisions for international corporations, who have the ability to exceed your sales goal tenfold with a single order. Or maybe you could meet with key influencers who could connect you with your ideal clients, so you're working with more warm leads on a regular basis. Or maybe you want to get an interview with a hiring manager to help land your dream job. Gaining access to the right people is the ultimate key to success. When you can do this, the possibilities are limitless!

That's what this book is all about. I will teach you how to get in front of whoever you want, whenever you want, for whatever reason you want. I realize that's a bold statement, but I'm a bold messenger and I have the stats to back it up. This will not be an easy road, but if you're willing to put in the work, you can transform your entire life.

Cold calling is hard. Over the years, millions have struggled through it with little success. Many think it's downright impossible.

For these reasons, many would say cold calling is dead. Don't believe that crap! I am here to tell you that cold calling is more alive than ever. And with so many people shying away from the cold call, there exists an even greater opportunity for those willing to put in the work.

By its nature, cold calling is hard. To compound the issue, the majority of training programs, common practices, and general advice tend to focus on the wrong things. The good news is I'm going to make it a lot easier for you. To start, there is no one-size-fits-all solution to cold calling. Everyone is unique. We all have different strengths, weaknesses, backgrounds, value systems, and quirks. The way we talk is different, the way we look at the world is different, and the way we form meaningful connections with others is different. We are once-for-all-time human beings, and there will never be another person just like us.

Considering that we're all so different, it's nuts to think a single script would work for everyone! And yet I see this expectation all the time. It's the norm at most companies. They give one script to their 400 sales professionals, who have 400 different sets of unique intangibles, and they expect similar results from everyone. It's not logical! Companies usually see their sales teams' results in a bell curve, and they think it's an indicator of talent; some people are just better at sales than others. When I go into companies and help with their cold calling, I see these results totally differently: the script simply fits some better than others.

When a script doesn't feel quite right to the salesperson, it's not going to sound quite right to the prospect. This should be obvious! When a pitch is awkward, how can we expect impressive results? Salespeople should not be forced to say things that don't feel natural to them. It doesn't help anyone—the company, the salesperson, or the prospect. It's about damn time to find a better way!

Depending on the stats you read and the research you examine, the average nationwide cold call success rate is about 6%.[1] I can't think of another profession on earth where that's acceptable. What if your doctor got your diagnosis right 6% of the time? What if your mechanic fixed your car properly 6% of the time? In any other position besides sales, if you were successful 6% of the time, you would be fired immediately and/or possibly even jailed for malpractice or fraud.

So, let's agree that the current way people are going about cold calling is completely wrong. To make a real impact, we need to blow this whole thing up and start over because we're going to need more than a little cosmetic tinkering. You don't want to go from 6% to 7%. You want to go from 6% to 67%. (That's the success rate Town Bank, a Wintrust Bank, experienced only two weeks after completing my Customized Group Cold Call Training program.[2] Jay Mack, the President & CEO of the bank, was so thrilled that I think he wanted to adopt me as his son!)

I have completely reinvented the cold-calling process, and this book presents an entirely new way forward, one you've never heard before. It's a step-by-step instruction manual to master the art and science of cold calling forever.

One of the best things about this process is that it looks a little different for everyone. I lay the foundation, and you fill in the blanks to personalize it and make it uniquely yours. Using this methodology, I will guide you through the process of creating a custom script that actually works for you—no matter who you work for or what you sell.

But this book won't only make you a world-class cold caller, it'll teach you how to build long-term relationships and influence. I wish I could take credit for this and say, "Yep, I designed it this way. I knew it all along!" But I didn't. I have been blown away by how these tools work almost universally in a variety of situations.

For example, if you can differentiate yourself and be memorable in a 20-second phone call, you can do that when you meet someone at a networking event, or write a follow-up email, or draft a direct mail piece. My methodology is based on human nature and psychology—not just phone calls. You will learn, among many other tips, how to pique curiosity and leave everyone you interact with wanting more. These skills transcend communication mediums!

Another beautiful thing about my methodology is it creates a sense of urgency. In sales, people can string you along forever. *"Call me next week." "Call me next quarter."* Tracking these conversations and following up wastes time. They don't really want to talk to you—they're just too polite to say it! If you can create urgency on a phone call, you can not only transform your success on the phone, you can influence people in a variety of situations. From job interviews to finally getting your spouse to work on that honey-do list, this book will teach you how to influence others to your way of thinking, while getting them to take quick action.

I am thrilled to take this journey with you! Think of me as your GPS. You're still in charge of driving the car—you decide how fast or slow to go, and you react to the other drivers on the road—but your GPS will keep you on track. That's how I'll help you. Throughout this book, you'll have the opportunity to personalize this journey and do all kinds of exercises, but it's up to you to actually do them. I'll be right here with you the whole time cheering you on, but you're driving!

With that in mind, let's shift this car into high gear!

Additional Resources

In this book, I break down the cold call building blocks as simply as possible, but when I teach this methodology in person, it's usually a several hour workshop. There is enough detail in this book to understand the crucial points and create your own script, but if you start to feel confused or stuck, you might want to check out my other resources to receive additional support.

In the spirit of this book, first I'll offer you a free way to get more content!

- **The Cold Call Coach YouTube Channel:** Check out my YouTube channel for a variety of videos on all kinds of information related to cold calling: http://youtube.com/c/TheColdCallCoach

- **Cold Call University:** If you're newer to cold calling, my online course is just what the doctor ordered! It's comprised of nine hours of content, covering all the fundamentals a salesperson needs to know. It's a comprehensive training program, and it consistently gets outstanding reviews. You can find it here: https://coldcallcoach.net/selling.

- **Cold Calling for Success Training System:** If you've been in sales for some time and your skills are more advanced, the Cold Calling for Success Training System is a great option. It's comprised of eight hours of content that focuses heavily on scripting, including how to leave great voicemails and the best ways to turn gatekeepers into advocates on your behalf. You can find it here: https://coldcallcoach.net/trainingsystem.

Key Terms

- **Person of Interest (POI):** The individuals with whom you aspire to secure dedicated time. Sometimes these people are the decision makers, but not always.

- **Center of Influence (COI):** The individuals who make a living from doing business with your ideal clients.

1

UNDERSTANDING THE COLD CALL

People often think the goal of cold calling is to dial total strangers and convince them to buy something immediately. They think that in those precious few seconds you get a Person of Interest (POI) on the phone, you should promote your company, explain why your products or services are needed, and make the sale, hanging up with a solid win in the books. Most of the time, this is unrealistic and ill-advised. And more importantly, it's diametrically opposed to how people buy in reality.

As human beings, we make decisions when we connect on a deep, emotive level. No one walks into a speed dating event and leaves an hour later engaged to be married. That would be a ludicrous expectation! When we're trying to meet our future partner, we have our eyes set on a single goal: getting a first date. We want quality one-on-one time to get to know the other person. From there, things will naturally play out and we'll see if we've found the right match. But trying to figure out if we've met our soul mate without truly getting to know the person is unrealistic.

When it comes to dating, most of us have our expectations in check. But when it comes to forming relationships through cold calling (and the sales process in general), our expectations often defy logic.

By nature, a cold call is the first time you connect with a POI. You've never met them, and they aren't expecting your call. No warm introduction from a mutual connection. They know nothing about you, and they likely don't know anything about your company. Total strangers.

To be successful, there can only be one goal during the cold call: to *get dedicated time with the POI.* That's it! If you meet this goal, consider your cold call a success.

Often, this surprises sales professionals. They've been taught a vastly different strategy. The sales industry typically defines cold calling success as some iteration of the following:

- Selling something

- Qualifying a POI

- Proactively building rapport (e.g., working hard to get them to like you)

These are all great, but they aren't what you should be focusing on during the cold call. Why? These goals have one thing in common: they turn the call, by nature, into a sales call. Think about it! You receive a call from a number you don't recognize. The person is someone you have never heard of who works for a company you are not familiar with. Your guard goes up. This total stranger is A) trying to sell something; B) asking you personal, qualifying questions; or C) trying to work hard to impress you for seemingly no reason. What kind of call must this be? A sales call! And when you realize you're suddenly on an unsolicited sales call with a total stranger, are you thrilled beyond belief? Are you eager to give generously of your time to hear this person out? Hardly! People don't like sales calls—even when salespeople can help them, save them money, make their lives better, and solve problems they didn't even know they had. Emotionally, they don't want anything to do with salespeople. It's a complete paradox!

That's why I believe that sales is neither a job nor a career. It's a vocation. It's something that, to be extremely successful in, you need to feel called to. Failing to make your numbers can mean not having enough money to pay the bills. You must love it because, on certain days, it's extremely difficult.

I've coached people so stressed out about their ability to perform that they were having panic attacks, crying under their desk before work, on the verge of quitting even though they had zero backup plan. I understand this struggle. I know how difficult the job can be. But there's no reason to make it harder than necessary! And when you're going after the three outcomes bulleted on the previous page (selling, qualifying, and/or building rapport), you're putting yourself at a major disadvantage because your POIs will automatically assume that they're on a sales call when they speak with you. Accordingly, they will try to end the call as quickly as possible, and your ability to procure dedicated time with them will be hampered dramatically.

As an example, imagine you have no idea who I am. Your phone rings. It's a number you don't recognize, but you elect to answer it anyway. This is what you hear on the other end of the phone:

- Hi, my name is Paul Neuberger, Founder & CEO of The Cold Call Coach. I just wanted to see if you're happy with your current cold call success rate.

Based upon my greeting, do you feel you have just found yourself in a sales call? If you're like just about everyone else with a pulse, you're now bracing yourself for a sales-related conversation and your mood goes down accordingly. In only two brief sentences, you already don't want to talk to me.

What, specifically, did I say that I was selling? Read the text again. I didn't say I was selling anything, but you automatically assumed this was the start of a sales call. It's that easy to self-incriminate, costing yourself valuable business development opportunities. What's the crime, you ask? Being a salesperson!

You may be expecting me to suggest you lie, manipulate, or be inauthentic to get what you want. But I promise that deviations from the truth are not a part of my proprietary methodology. However, you will need to do something radically different, or you're never going to get out of the batter's box on your cold calls.

In this book, I will teach you to build a script that makes POIs want to keep talking. Our goal is to get dedicated time with POIs, and your new script will enable you to schedule more meetings with them than ever before.

This isn't a one-size-fits-all script. That would never work. Instead, my step-by-step formula will guide you through the five building blocks of a world-class cold call. You will learn the purpose of each part of the script, and the kinds of information you should share with POIs to differentiate yourself and create a sense of urgency. We'll also cover how to handle gatekeepers and craft effective voicemail scripts that will blow your current callback rate out of the water.

My program works because it provides direction and parameters. Don't be like the hamster running in its wheel, endlessly churning and getting nowhere. Instead of trying to figure it out through trial and error, my methodology gives you the strategy and structure to systematically move forward.

Get Ready for Your Transformation

As a sales guy, I like to have quantifiable metrics to measure performance. Whenever I work with clients, I record their numbers two weeks after finishing my training program so we can gain a better understanding of improvement. These metrics are proof that my program doesn't just work—it's absolutely transformative!

Everyone has different starting points, and it's impossible to do an apples-to-apples comparison to other individuals or organizations, but it can be inspiring to know what kinds of results others are getting. Here are a few examples:

- An international manufacturing company with hundreds of employees all over the world got in touch with me soon after they decided to incorporate cold calling into their sales team's business strategy. Most of their sales team was in their mid to late 20s, and they had little training or experience in cold calling. When I began working with them, they had virtually zero success closing any business from cold calls. Within two weeks, the team had scheduled dedicated time with 50% of the POIs they spoke with on the phone.

- I also worked with Town Bank, a Wintrust Bank, which is comprised of very experienced sales professionals who have been cold calling for a long time. Town Bank hires well and they have a solid group, but they brought me in to present a fresh perspective. Within two weeks, their sales team had a 67% cold call success rate, and 42% callback rate for their voicemails, making them one of the top-performing organizations I have ever had the privilege to train.

- I worked with an international sign and advertising franchise that has 661 locations across the country. Their Wisconsin team had varying degrees of experience. In my Group Training Program, I usually dedicate a portion of the agenda to doing live cold calls. Salespeople take turns calling POIs while their colleagues watch and learn. One woman was very nervous, and she made her first cold call during this portion of the training. She was able to schedule an appointment, and within 30 days, she had closed $45,000 in new business. From her very first cold call!

- I conducted my Group Cold Call Training Program on a small team of professionals at KI, which is headquartered in Green Bay, Wisconsin. KI is a world-class company specializing in workplace furniture solutions. All five participants in the program were new to both the organization and sales in general. None of them had ever cold called prior to my arrival. Within two weeks, their cold call success rate was 38.9%, and their voicemail response rate was 21.2%.

- Several years ago I worked with an organization in Cincinnati, Ohio, that specialized in professional audiovisual system integration. That's where I met the biggest skeptic I've ever trained. We'll call him Greg. Greg was against the program from the start. He thought he was good enough at his job and that he didn't need to change anything. I started earning his respect when I coached the team on leaving better voicemails, but he still sulked his way through the beginning of the training. Greg said he had left hundreds of voicemails and never had anyone call him back. During the live training, he left a voicemail using the new script that we developed together. He executed it well, and as we were talking through his message and what he'd done correctly, his phone rang. Sure enough, it was the guy he had just called. Greg went back into his cold call script and scheduled an appointment right then. After that, I had Greg's buy in. Over the next few years, he found more success as a sales professional than he ever expected and became one of my biggest supporters.

While results vary across sales professionals and organizations, my clients continuously find an enormous amount of success once they adopt my methodology. They meet with POIs more frequently, close bigger pieces of business, and speed up the sales cycle to close more deals faster than ever before. But most importantly, my clients are empowered to take control of their businesses and livelihoods.

Before reading this book, you might have thought, "If only I could get in front of the right person." Now you can! "If only," are the two worst words in the human language. They limit you and confine your ability to succeed. I believe it's my calling in life to liberate you from those restraints.

2

IDENTIFYING IDEAL CLIENTS

We go through life seeking quality. We want our kids to go to quality schools, we work to develop quality relationships, and we want to live in quality homes. We spend money to put a quality dinner on the table instead of 300 Hostess cakes to achieve maximum caloric density for the price.

But when it comes to cold calling, something strange happens in our brains where we instinctively assume that quantity is better than quality. Instead of making a few extremely targeted calls, many salespeople make hundreds, if not thousands of calls hoping a handful, if they're lucky, lead to business.

Wouldn't it be great if you could focus only on your *ideal clients*, those individuals, organizations, or entities that have a heightened sense of urgency for your products or services right now *and* who will pay you very well?

You may be thinking, "Oh sure, that sounds great, but there's no way to know who your ideal clients are before you actually talk to them." I used to think the same thing—until I realized a better way. In this chapter, I will show you how you can not only define your ideal clients, but go beyond basic demographics and traditional methods for qualifying leads to see what other salespeople are constantly missing.

When I first started working as a financial associate selling insurance and helping people manage their money, I was given a long list of unqualified leads, some basic scripts, and was told to have at it. (As you probably well know, this is the standard routine at most sales organizations, with salespeople expected to dial for dollars.) With all that time on the phone, I quickly learned that certain demographics of POIs were much more likely to want to do business with me *right then*. I also noticed that certain demographics of POIs would make me a lot more money in commission than others, just based on what their needs were.

Being an ambitious guy, I figured I would have the best chance at success if I learned how to spend my time wisely. I decided to identify the conditions that gave me the best shot at closing lucrative deals as quickly as possible. I thought long and hard, consulted several of my colleagues, and came up with the following six criteria:

- **Men:** They tended to be more hands-off than women, so I had more freedom to design their entire financial plan.

- **Age 45–60:** They had worked long enough to have accumulated wealth and were closer to retirement, therefore the urgency tension among them was higher than young people.

- **Lived within 25 miles of my office:** We could easily meet in person and cultivate our relationship.

- **Changed jobs at least twice in the last 25 years:** They had money in different places from 401(k)s and other work-related accounts, which gave me the opportunity to help them consolidate.

- **Right in the middle of a divorce:** Their financial world has been turned upside down and they need to come up with a new plan quickly.

- **Would get at least $1M after the divorce:** This meant a sizeable commission for me.

Out of this whole list, divorce was the thing that turned POIs into customers more effectively and efficiently than the rest. Going through a divorce is a major life event—albeit, an unfortunate one. Life events are the ultimate timing mechanism for closing sales because they create a sense of urgency for POIs. People can string you along for weeks, months, or even years if they don't have the urgency to buy, but a life event makes them get their butts in gear. Life events also change people's perspectives, making certain products or services much more important in their lives than they once were.

I was glad to have finally identified my ideal clients, and quite frankly, I felt like a genius for recognizing the value of life events. I remember telling a colleague that I had uncovered the key to becoming more successful at sales. He immediately burst my bubble when he asked, "That's great, Paul, but how are you going to find these people?"

My heart sank. I knew he was right. It's not like men walk around with a "back on the market" sign hanging from their neck. I felt like I was back at square one. Was

I doomed to play "the numbers game" and keep dialing until my fingers grew callouses? I was determined to avoid that. I needed to find my ideal clients—fast. For weeks, I couldn't think of anything else as I obsessed over this matter incessantly.

Finally, I had an epiphany. My ideal clients would need support from others at this critical time in their lives, such as divorce attorneys, real estate agents, and marriage counselors—among others. There had to be tons of local divorce attorneys, real estate agents, etc. who were already in contact with my ideal clients, essentially making a living off this very same life event. These individuals became my Centers of Influences (COIs). If I could build relationships with some of these COIs, perhaps their clients could become my clients. Of course, I could have cold called them and said, "Introduce me to your clients so I can sell to them too," but as dense as I can be sometimes, even I realized that wasn't the best idea. If I wanted to get in good with these people, I would need to develop meaningful relationships with them.

Instead of wasting precious time continuing to dial for dollars, I spent the next few days researching divorce attorneys. I identified them as the most prominent COIs that I wanted to build rapport with. I looked through their websites and LinkedIn profiles and identified a handful that seemed to work with clients who matched as many of my six criteria as possible. I figured that the best way to approach these COIs would be to offer something of value without asking anything in return. That's just plain logic. And since we had similar target markets, it stood to reason that maybe I could refer them business as well. So, I picked up the phone and my script went something like this:

> Good morning, Karen. Paul Neuberger. I hope you're having a great day! I want to learn more about your legal services. I may have some clients to send your way. As a local financial advisor, I work with individuals who, regrettably, go through divorce from time to time. I obsess about bringing value to my clients and want to help them address their every need. I would love to stop by, learn more about your practice, and see if you might be a good extension of my business.

And what do you know? Not wanting to turn down a potential source of referrals to grow their businesses, nearly all those individuals agreed to meet with me. In fact, I had more than 50 COI meetings scheduled within the first couple weeks of implementing this new methodology. You read that correctly!

Since I was on those appointments to learn about their businesses, I asked a lot of questions. I was interested in getting to know them, but I was also qualifying them as a source of referrals for my business. (Did they actually do business with my ideal clients? Obviously, that would make a difference in how I pursued the relationship moving forward.) That said, I still made it my top priority to put them first and help them out, as I said I would in my cold call.

If I didn't have any clients to refer at that moment, I made an effort to help in other ways. Sometimes I offered them a recommendation on LinkedIn or shared a status update that would promote them within my network, just in case anyone I knew was in the market for their services. Other times I invited them to a networking event my company was hosting or sent an email introducing them to a friend or colleague they might be interested in meeting.

Paying it forward is a worthwhile thing to do, and I was happy to extend those offers without any expectation that they would reciprocate. But I was surprised that with just about every single new relationship, people asked what they could do for me in return. The more I gave, the more I got!

Using my new method, I was earning a six-figure salary by the time I was 31. (That might not sound like a lot to some of you, but living in a small town in Wisconsin, that money went pretty far!) The best part was I continued growing my network at breakneck speed. This led to more and more referrals, further lessening my need to cold call people who were not my ideal clients.

When my sales numbers started skyrocketing, my boss and the rest of the sales team demanded to know what on earth had happened. How did I go from being average to absolutely crushing all expectations? This was my first step in transitioning from being a sales guy to becoming a sales trainer. I started teaching my colleagues how to do what I was doing, and they all saw how well it worked. Identifying ideal clients wasn't the only thing I was doing that contributed to my success, but it became a cornerstone in getting an opportunity to use my other sales skills in front of the right people.

VOLUME-BASED SELLING VS. RELATIONAL SELLING:

Depending on what you're selling, how much it costs, and how much you earn in commission per sale, your business is either skewed toward volume (quantity of sales) or relationships. Although the ideal client method is essential for relational selling, it's also useful for volume selling. If you are expected to call a certain number of leads every day, having a deeper understanding of your ideal clients will help you better qualify your leads, more efficiently use your time, and close more deals faster than ever before. It's also important to note that many sales organizations use a volume-based approach because they haven't figured out how to target their ideal clients. Using my proven method of connecting with COIs has helped numerous sales organizations transform their approach to find even greater success from relational selling.

Exercise - Identify your ideal clients

Now that you understand the power of ideal clients, it's time for you to define your own. You probably already have a couple thoughts in mind, but I want you to ensure that all criteria are quantifiable and objective. This gives you specifics to look for so you can easily recognize your ideal clients when you see them; there's no grey area. For example, you aren't simply looking for "big" companies. Instead, you're looking for companies with more than a thousand employees. Take your time, dig deep, and put some serious thought and consideration into this matter. The more time you take upfront to complete this task, the less time you will need to monetize these opportunities when you start calling them.

Now, you may be thinking, "Won't six requirements mean I have a very narrow group of people to target?" Yes! That's the point. After years of testing this process and working with thousands of sales professionals, I've found that six appears to be the magic number to get to the heart of your target market. Instead of contacting all kinds of POIs, these six conditions will allow you to identify people who need you *right now*. You shouldn't be going through the back of the church directory and calling 600 families. How many of those individuals need your services *right now*? Only a tiny fraction. As a result, you must endure hundreds of calls that waste your most precious commodity: time. If you're spending time selling to people who don't need your products or services, you're drastically limiting your ability to be successful.

Think about it as a triangle. With each of your six criteria you narrow your field of POIs and move down toward the tip so that when you get to the bottom of the triangle you're left with only high-quality POIs.

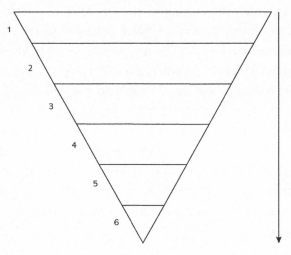

Of your six requirements, make one a life event. Since this is the most important part of making this process work, you need to pick the right one to ensure your success. Here are some examples:

- **B2B life events:** New HR manager, personnel changes, merger or acquisition, safety incident, OSHA violation, corporate expansion, award or recognition, enlargement of physical footprint, opening of another office, hiring or downsizing a significant number of employees, ending a contract with another vendor

- **B2C life events:** Marriage, divorce, new baby, kids starting college, moving, starting a new job, changing careers, going back to school, beginning to take care of elderly relatives, death of a loved one, buying a new car, retiring, a health or medical issue

Take your time to define your ideal clients and reflect on what's worked for you in the past. Review your previous sales to identify those that closed quickly and carefully examine opportunities that ended up being big wins for you. Brainstorm on where the commonalities lie. You might spot similarities you hadn't noticed before. Also make sure to talk with colleagues and/or your boss about their own experiences and how they target and identify their ideal clients.

If you sell a variety of solutions, you should also consider whether you like selling certain products or services better than others. When you have passion for what you're selling, you're going to have more enthusiasm and success, which enables you to sell even more. Consider focusing your efforts on what you enjoy selling. The positive impact it can have on your efforts will snowball, gaining unstoppable momentum!

If you're having trouble identifying a life event to target, don't give up or settle on something that's merely OK. Sometimes when I'm working with sales teams, people say they don't have a life event associated with their ideal clients. This is never the case. Don't get me wrong; it's not easy. I've had a lot of practice over the years and I've spent what probably amounts to an absurd amount of time thinking about ideal clients, but I want you to know that your answer is out there. Don't give up!

Exercise - Identify your COIs

Once you've identified your ideal life event, you're ready to target your COIs. The best COIs don't just make money from your life event—they make their living off it. You want to find people who work with your ideal clients day in and day out, providing a product or service that does not compete with what you're selling.

- For B2B life events, you might consider targeting corporate recruiters, high-level business coaches, crisis consultants, corporate attorneys, relocation firms, commercial real estate agents, or commercial architecture or design firms.

- For B2C life events, you could consider options like life coaches, insurance providers, financial advisors, real estate agents, retirement homes, daycare centers, recruiters, physical therapists, home health companies, doulas and prenatal care professionals, and adult education workers.

COIs are easier to get in front of than your ideal clients, and they are the gift that keeps on giving. If you can develop good relationships with the right COIs, you'll have a steady stream of referrals coming in and you won't have to make as many cold calls. This essentially switches the nature of your role from being in *sales* to *facilitation*. Your POI knows they have a need, they are just looking for someone to fill it. You don't have to be a genius to recognize that facilitation is easier than sales!

Take some time and be thoughtful about choosing your COIs, but don't stress over it. Some salespeople think this part is too hard and revert to simply calling anyone and everyone. Don't do that! There's an easier way to find your ideal clients, but you must put in the work to see the results.

Start with one or two types of COIs and then research the real-life people you can contact. You can use online resources like LinkedIn and Google, or ask your personal network for introductions. Use the sample script I provided earlier in the chapter and follow the same approach. Just like cold calling customers, the key here is adding value. When you say you might have people to refer to your COIs, it's true. It's not gimmicky; it's strategic networking. People join membership groups, city chamber organizations, or go to alumni events to connect with peers and close more business. This is just a more targeted way to collaborate and network.

Depending on what you're selling, your COIs might even end up becoming your clients. Over the years, numerous times an attorney or real estate agent in my network expressed an interest in moving money from an old 401(k) or exploring new investments, and since they had met me in person and thought I was a nice guy, they felt comfortable hiring me. Although they weren't my "ideal" clients when it came to cold calling, if the defense gives you a layup, take the layup! I wouldn't have spent time chasing these opportunities, but I'll always take an easy basket.

Through the years, I've developed close relationships with a lot of the COIs I met. Some have become good family friends. I share this so you know that finding your COIs isn't a manipulative act that's based on ulterior motives. It's about forming strategic partnerships to improve your organization and increase your success, both professionally and personally. Imagine if all business transactions were conducted in this manner!

It's time to work smarter, not harder! No matter what you're currently selling, becoming a student of this process is going to make you more effective. It is a true blessing to partake in this game-changing journey with you.

3

PEOPLE BUY PEOPLE, NOT COMPANIES

A key reason why I have been so successful at cold calling is because no matter what product or service I'm selling, I'm actually selling *myself*. That's right! Who knew that people would want to buy a loud, high-octane guy with a ridiculously prominent forehead (I've been told that I have a face for cold calling)? I've taught thousands of salespeople across the United States and around the world how to get dedicated time with anyone by selling themselves instead of their company. In this chapter, I will teach you how to do the same.

To get started, think about your sales script. Reflect on what you typically say to a potential customer on that first call. Don't try to change it for the purpose of this exercise! Recite your normal script out loud and then record it with your cellphone or write it down.

OK, now let me ask you this question. Do people buy people first or do people buy companies first? Even if you think it's a combination of both, pick the one you think is most influential.

When I ask this question in front of large groups of people, at least 95% say that people buy people first—not companies. Why? Because you want to work with someone you like! Someone you trust. Someone you have something in common with who makes you feel comfortable. POIs buy from you when they feel good about you. This is something that people universally understand. Yet for most sales professionals, there's a disconnect between what they believe and what they say. Somehow during the cold call process, they forget everything they've ever learned about human interaction.

Now, refer back to your cold call script. What are you saying to your POIs? Are you selling yourself as a human being first? I can almost guarantee that you are leading with your company, the services you provide, the products you sell, the professional value you offer, etc. That's why you aren't getting 15 appointments from 15 cold calls. You're leading with something that people don't buy first! Becoming more successful is as easy as changing your approach.

Some salespeople will push back, saying, "But Paul, people are ultimately buying the products or services the company is providing. The company has to be able to deliver." And they're right! The quality of what you're selling matters. And at some point you need to sell the company. But we're talking about cold calls here. First impressions. And you know what? The messenger matters more than the message. The way to get dedicated time with someone is to make them like you. You can sell the company later. And unless the company is stealing from people, killing puppies, or committing some other atrocity, the facts about the organization will not matter as much as how people feel about *you*.

In every industry, people buy people before they buy companies. That's why non-compete agreements exist! People will follow their financial advisor, their doctor, and their realtor, among many others, wherever they go. Maybe you think selling is different. Trust me, it's not. Even if your current position is more of a volume-based sales role, you still have a better shot at closing more sales if you focus on selling yourself before you sell your company.

Intangibles

The best way to sell yourself is to put your intangibles on prominent display. Intangibles are the basket of traits you were born with that cannot be taught in any classroom, such as humor, honesty, and charisma. You have enhanced and refined these qualities throughout your life, from the environment you grew up in and your experiences along the way. Intangibles are the unique qualities that make clients fall in love with you as an individual. They give you a competitive advantage no matter what industry you're in or what you're selling.

As mentioned above, intangibles cannot be taught. As an example, knowledge is not an intangible. Anyone can gain knowledge if they work at it. Experience is not an intangible either. A chimpanzee can be on the job for 20 years, but that doesn't mean the experience is automatically a benefit to you if you choose to work with that chimp. Intangibles are best described as *how* you go about your work.

How would you feel about working with someone who has a good sense of humor and can always bring a smile to your face? What about someone who does what he says he's going to do and always follows through? What about someone who is dedicated to always providing you with the very best experience and exceeding your expectations? Those people sound great, right? Wouldn't you want to work with those individuals, whether they were your go-to people for your company's office supplies, handled your tax returns, or performed your annual physical?

I'm going to teach you how to incorporate your intangibles into your cold call script so that you can better sell yourself as a human being. But to be able to put your intangibles on display, you need to first determine what they are.

Exercise - Identify five intangibles

What makes you special, unique, and quite frankly, better to work with than others selling similar products or services? Ask your spouse, your coworkers, your friends, and your clients what qualities set you apart. Your goal is to identify five intangibles.

Here's my list as an example:

- **Integrity** - I say what I mean, and I do what I say. Period.

- **Humor** - I have a light-hearted approach that makes people laugh. (Sometimes with me, sometimes at me.)

- **Empathy** - I'm a little embarrassed to admit this, but I tear up rather readily. Even TV commercials have been known to make my eyes water.

- **Charisma** - I'm enthusiastic about the things I care about, and it can't help but shine through!

- **Energetic** - My brain feels like it's moving at a million miles per hour, and the rest of me can't help but follow.

I did not come up with this list overnight. It took time, self-reflection, and many conversations with the people who know me best.

Give your list the attention it deserves. Jot down some ideas now but know that you'll need to refine your list as you talk to people and gain their insight. As you home in on some potential intangibles, make sure to be honest with yourself. This is not the time to jot down characteristics you *wish* you had. If your list of intangibles is not authentic, you will have a harder time incorporating them into your script.

To demonstrate the awesome power of intangibles and how well they work in a setting such as cold calling, I've devised a quick test. Come up with three professions totally unrelated to yours. The further removed the better. Now imagine you are in need of someone from each of these fields. You ask a friend, "Do you know of a good X?" Let's say a doctor. They reply:

> *Yes, I know a great doctor! I can always count on her. She doesn't recommend drugs I don't need and doesn't make me come in for every little thing just so she can bill my insurance. She's always cracking jokes and puts me in a good mood even when I'm sick. She's a great listener, and I can tell she really cares about me. She's also very enthusiastic in her suggestions for helping*

me improve my health, and I can tell she really enjoys working with patients. She's always going above and beyond when I have questions or concerns. I don't know where she finds all that energy!

Would you want to make an appointment with this doctor? I sure as heck would! This recommendation puts her intangibles on display and paints a clear picture of who this person is and why she's valuable to patients. In just a few sentences, you feel like you know her. You can probably even picture yourself as her patient.

Try this exercise using your own intangibles to describe three different professionals, as I did with the doctor above. Do you feel the same about the people you described as you did with the doctor? If so, you know you've identified the right qualities. If not, you should do a little more brainstorming to come up with the perfect list of five intangibles. We will use this list later in the book to develop your custom cold-calling script, so please complete this exercise before then.

> Your intangibles will make a difference in your ability to get dedicated time with POIs during the cold call, but this is truly a long-term strategy that should redefine all interactions with everyone you encounter moving forward. Find new, innovative, and different ways to bring out your intangibles. Over time, it will become a part of your muscle memory and Sales DNA, ensuring execution without even thinking about it.

The science behind emotional buying

Intangibles are essential to cold calling success because they strike an emotional chord with POIs. As human beings, we are wired to act on our emotions rather than logic. It isn't weakness; it's physiological, and it's tied to our ability to survive.

The brain is divided into sections specializing in different functions. The amygdala, a more primitive part, deals with our fight or flight response. Sometimes referred to as "the lizard brain," its primary purpose is to keep us alive. When our ancestors encountered a sabre-toothed tiger, the amygdala would kick in with the "fight or flight" response. Do we stay and fight the beast, or do we turn around and run like hell? Knowing that we face a potentially life-threatening encounter either way, our heart rate gets jacked up, blood flow increases to our extremities, our pupils dilate, and our senses become enhanced—all to give us the very best chance of surviving this harrowing situation.

To this day, it's still the part of the brain that protects us and gives us the best chance of survival in dangerous situations. When the amygdala is activated, we see and hear things better, we react quicker. If we see someone trapped under a car (God forbid), it's the part of our brain that will help us miraculously find the strength to lift it up and save that person.

The prefrontal cortex serves a much different purpose, and it is a more recent addition to the human brain from an evolutionary perspective. It developed when our ancestors started living in groups and communicating with one another in more complex ways, and it is one of the greatest physiological differences between us and animals. The prefrontal cortex enables us to understand complex scenarios, regulate social behavior, express personality, and understand consequences. It drives "higher" brain functions and is synonymous with logic, reasoning, and the processing of information.

So, no matter how much we want to focus on logic in our sales pitches and presentations, physiologically, it's nearly impossible to override emotional responses within the brain. That's why salespeople have greater success when they focus on activating people's emotions, rather than their logic.

Sales professionals wonder all the time why POIs don't buy from them. Maybe they could save someone hundreds of dollars a month, make their processes more efficient, or provide more coverage for a fraction of the cost. Why won't the POI buy their solution? Time and time again across a range of industries and situations, POIs don't pull the trigger. It's not logical! In these situations, the POI is often thinking to themselves, "I know this would save me money, but it doesn't feel right." Or, "This would be good for my business, but I'm just not excited about it." To avoid putting yourself in situations like this, always try to create an emotional response during your cold calls, as well as in all future interactions.

When I'm connecting with POIs, clients, COIs, colleagues, friends—or really anyone for that matter—I want to drive an emotional conversation. The topics can be about anything: their kids, the Milwaukee Brewers, or the amazing restaurant they went to last week. Whatever we're talking about, I put my intangibles on display, and I try to make people feel good. When I'm meeting with people in person, I measure my success at driving these emotional conversations by how often people smile, nod their head, and whether they lean forward in their chair wanting to hear more.

Taking a similar approach to your communications will drive more interesting and meaningful conversations. It will also make it easier to build quality relationships faster.

Another major benefit is getting more passionate referrals from your network—especially your COIs. Let's go back to the previous example of the recommendation for a doctor. Suppose you asked another friend, and he stuck to the facts about the company instead of highlighting the doctor's intangibles:

> *Yes, I know a great doctor! She has experience treating a wide range of health conditions. She's part of ABC Medical practice, which is a great consortium of physicians. They have been in business for 10 years serving people of all ages across the community. They accept a bunch of different insurance providers, and you can make appointments by calling or emailing. They're very punctual and they keep the office clean. It's also very easy to park there.*

This recommendation is extremely positive, but it doesn't strike an emotional chord like the first one did. That's a major problem! Why? *People won't always remember what you said, but they'll never forget how they felt when you said it.*

Let's imagine two weeks have gone by since getting both recommendations, and you've finally found the time to reach out to a doctor and make an appointment. Which doctor would you call? Chances are, you would choose the first one. I know I would! That recommendation painted a picture in my mind of an ideal doctor. I pictured the doctor going above and beyond to help my friend, and I even pictured myself as a patient. This is the emotional brain in action. My memories about this recommendation are sticky because they activated my emotions.

The second recommendation was positive, but vanilla. Hearing the facts didn't strike an emotional chord, and because of that, it didn't paint a vivid picture in my head. As a result, I'm less likely to remember the details later and pursue the recommendation.

It is important to keep in mind, since you should be planning on getting a lot of business from referrals. If you strike a deep, emotional chord with your COIs, it'll come through in their recommendations to their network.

4

HOW TO INSTANTANEOUSLY DIFFERENTIATE YOURSELF AND BE MEMORABLE

Like many business buzz words, a lot of lip service is given to differentiation. When you can stand out from the competition, it's easier to bring in new business—and keep it. Unfortunately, the execution is oftentimes lacking.

Imagine you are sitting down with your ideal client. Not just any ideal client, but your number-one whale. You're at the company's corporate headquarters, sitting in the main conference room at a 50-foot table. There are many leather-bound books and the room smells of rich mahogany. Your C-suite POI (the woman who makes all the decisions) says:

> *I want to know the one thing that we will get from working with your organization that we cannot find with any other company on the planet. No matter how many websites we read, LinkedIn profiles we examine, reference checks we conduct, prospectuses we pour over, or conversations we have with your competitors, what will we be unable to find anywhere else? What is the one thing you have that no one else has?*

At this point, you may be wondering if you should fake a medical emergency to stall for more time. Or maybe the thought of not having a good answer and losing the deal of a lifetime is enough to spontaneously induce a medical emergency! If you can keep it together, how would you answer? Would you say something about how you have a great team that truly cares about clients? Or that your customer service is top-notch? Maybe you'd talk about your product being the best in the industry?

Here's where I play the role of Jerk Paul. He likes to poke holes in ideas. If Jerk Paul had asked for a single differentiating factor and got an answer like the above, he would say something sarcastic like:

> I can't believe my luck! Maybe I should go out and buy a lotto ticket! Out of all the companies I could have sat down with today, I can't believe I found the only one that takes care of its clients! You mean to tell me that all of the other organizations would treat me like dirt, but yours is the only one that will respect me and treat me with the dignity that I deserve?

The problem is people try to answer this question with *what* their organization does: "This is what we do. This is what we provide. This is what we offer. This is what makes us unique." This will never truly be a differentiating factor. Even if it feels as unique as a snowflake to you, you will not be able to successfully convey that message to your POIs because at least one other organization on Earth can answer this question in the same manner that you can. Aside from that, *what* you do will not hit your POIs at a deep, emotive level, which means it won't be memorable, nor is it likely to compel your prospective buyers to take action quickly.

Instead of focusing on the "what," homing in on the "how" will get you a step closer to successful differentiation. What's one thing POIs will only get working with your organization? You! With this in mind, "how" you work with clients digs a little deeper. You're funny and driven and caring, and that's how you help your clients. Plus, describing to your POIs, in detail, how you will serve them and what your interactions will look like moving forward hits them at a deeper, more emotive level, which is great because people are emotional buyers, not logical buyers. As wonderful as all of this is, however, millions of people share these qualities with you, so if you are not the only one who possesses this, it cannot technically be considered differentiation.

To truly differentiate yourself as a salesperson, you must go deeper still. Instead of leading with the "what" or the "how," to effectively stand alone amongst all of humanity, you must lead with your Why.

The power of Why

Author Simon Sinek launched a movement from the idea that everyone has profound reasons for doing the things they do. These motivations are why people get out of bed every day, why they push to do their best at work, and why they see the world the way they do. Sinek gives sage advice when he says, "People don't buy WHAT you do; they buy WHY you do it."[3] This insight has become a core part of leadership development for many individuals and companies because it really gets to the heart of motivation. By identifying your Why, you can harness your own inspiration, encourage others with your story, and be memorable—all of which are great for salespeople!

This is precisely the reason I always lead with my Why. At the beginning of this book, I introduced myself. I told you a little bit about who I am and why I originally got into sales working as a financial advisor. As you likely recall, my father-in-law died unexpectedly, and my family went through unnecessary financial hardship because the proper insurance policies were not in place. I tell this story at the beginning of all my keynotes and workshops because it helps people understand what I've gone through and what motivates me every day. But I don't just give the high-level overview of this story; I give the details as I experienced them. I paint a picture so people feel like they were in the room with my father-in-law when this event took place.

When I share this story with audiences, there are always a few people who tear up. Why? Is it because I'm a world-class storyteller? Is it because I'm the most articulate guy around? Hardly. Maybe they also lost a loved one suddenly. Or they are thinking about how painful it would be if they went through the same thing that my family did. When people have a deep, emotional response to a story, it becomes memorable. That's why audiences are able to recall every little detail hours, days, weeks, even months later: My father-in-law died of a heart attack. He had only recently become a grandfather. He was putting on his socks when it happened. He died on his 60th birthday.

Think about how different the impact would be if I led with the What instead of the Why when explaining getting my start in sales: "I became a financial advisor because I wanted to protect people's assets via innovative insurance modalities and guarantee a bright financial future through sound fiscal planning."

Who's going to care about that or remember it months down the road? It's not interesting or memorable because it sounds like every other financial advisor on the planet. To truly set yourself apart, you have to lead with your Why.

You may be wondering how to fit your Why into your cold calls. Obviously, you can't dump your entire life story on POIs within a few seconds of them picking up the phone. But I'm going to show you how to give POIs a taste of your story and leave them wanting more. It's just like the free samples at the food court in the mall. You might not have been thinking about Chinese food, but as soon as you get a taste of that General Tso's chicken, you just have to go back for the full plate. It's the exact same effect you're going for with the cold call. And although we'll only be using a tiny portion of the whole story around your Why in our script, you need to develop the entire story before we can trim it down. The good news is that once you put in the work on your Why, it can be used in a variety of situations, including email marketing, direct mail, and speaking with POIs in person.

Exercise - Developing your Why

Developing your Why can be a surprisingly complex task. Start by reflecting on the following questions. Read through them now and keep thinking about them over the course of the coming days:

- Why do you go to work every morning? You can get a paycheck at any job, so why do you choose to stay with this one?

- Why are you passionate about your work?

- What makes you excited to go to work?

- Why do you stay in the line of work you're in?

- What about your company gives you the most pride?

- How have past jobs made you appreciate your current role even more?

- What makes you smile at work?

- What would you miss most about your job if you lost it?

- How does your job enable you to leverage your skills and talents to be the best possible version of yourself?

Your Story

Don't expect to have all these answers right away. But when you do get some clarity, begin to figure out a way to build an interesting story around your answers. Stories help people see what you see and experience what you experienced. A good story is in narrative form and doesn't just state the facts. For example, "I like people" is not a story and would not be considered a viable Why statement.

In some cases, you'll have a specific moment in time that defines your Why and made you look at life differently.

Think of your own major life events. (A health scare, the death of a loved one, something that shocked you, a special achievement, etc.) Perhaps you've had a long-standing belief and you're looking for a moment to bring it to life. If you love your job because your boss and coworkers are like family members, how could you express that with a single example?

Sometimes you need to build up and amplify the little things to tell them in a big way. Does this mean you're dramatizing your Why? Perhaps to a certain degree. But it takes bigger convictions to sway people. This does not mean you should lie to make a boring story more exciting. But you may need to work harder to understand why your story is interesting.

Here is the proprietary five-step process I created with respect to developing a world-class story around your Why and making you memorable to everyone you speak with:

- **Add details and specifics.** Just like a mountain climber with crampons, details give people something to hang on to and store for future recall. Additionally, when you add detailed specifics to your story, on a psychological level, you start sucking people in and, soon, they are hanging on your every word.

    It reminds me of something that happened to me recently. I don't sleep much. Not because I can't, but because I won't. I simply want to get as much out of each day as possible. But when I do sleep, I sleep heavy. I'm basically in a coma, truthfully. So, I rarely wake up before my alarm goes off at 3:30am. The other night I woke up at 1:45am. That never happens! Worse yet, I had a sense of foreboding; a heaviness. I felt like something was terribly wrong and it only got worse as time slowly dragged on. I tossed and turned, said a prayer, heck, I even tried counting sheep (does anybody still do that these days?), but couldn't go back to sleep. I finally decided I had to get up. I descended the stairs, went straight to the kitchen and flipped on the light, illuminating the room. It was then that my worst fears were realized.

This is actually a made-up story about me waking up in the middle of the night, but the details sucked you in like a vacuum cleaner! When I tell it in person, I take a lot of pauses and speak in a dramatic fashion. All the nuances and specifics bring the story to life and set a very specific emotional tone. That's what you want to do with your Why!

- **Elicit an emotional response.** People are emotional buyers. If you don't elicit an emotional response in your story, you're at a huge disadvantage with respect to making yourself memorable. But luckily, your story can elicit any emotion—happiness, sadness, frustration, embarrassment, etc. Just make the other person truly feel something!

- **Present conflict.** This is the only criteria on the list that isn't a deal breaker when creating your Why because, quite frankly, not everyone's story has a conflict component associated with it. That said, you should aspire to present conflict because it humanizes you and enhances your credibility with the POI. Conflict also makes for a more interesting story. Think about the best-selling movies of all time. Would the *Jurassic Park* franchise have had anywhere near the same level of success if the dinosaurs never escaped?

- **Discuss your transformation.** How are you different now because of the conflict you experienced? How does it tie to your story overall? When you can describe how your experience changed you, it foreshadows the change your client can expect when they decide to work with you.

- **Make a connection between your story and the POI.** Without this step, all you have is a good story. It just takes one sentence at the very end of your narrative to make this connection. Here's an example of how I've done this in the story about my Why: "My family has had to experience firsthand how unnecessarily difficult life can be if you don't plan in advance, and I would hate for your family to experience the same thing."

Examples of World-Class Why Stories

These five steps sound great in theory, but it can be hard to know how to put these elements together without examples. Here are a few of my favorites:

Example 1 - Banking: When I worked with the Town Bank, a Wintrust Bank, sales team, I met Dan Brenton, an individual with a life-long passion for banking. From a very early age, he knew he would be a banker, and he built his story around that. He talked about how his parents, who owned and managed several businesses, would often take him with them into the bank as a child. He will never forget the smell of the lobby! His parents would put him on the marble counter, and he could feel the cold on the back of his legs. He loved playing with the pens, which were attached to the counters by those metallic chains. The tellers would always hand him a crisp $100 bill just to see the expression on his little face. He would hold the bill, breathe it in, and his parents would tell him how people work very hard for their money and that the bank helps keep it safe. He was hooked.

There was a brief time in college where he fought his natural inclination to go into banking. It was a way to rebel against his own personal expectations of himself and choose a different path. But it turned out that he didn't love the new course he had charted for his life, and he wasn't passionate about it. So, after a few years, he decided to follow his heart and go into banking after all. He realized how much he missed the bank environment, and he never wavered again. His Why shows that banking is a vocation for him, which evokes a sense of trust from POIs and customers.

Example 2 - Insurance: Ashley Johnson is a Group Benefits Producer at The Starr Group, and she has an extremely powerful Why. She grew up on her family farm, got married on the property, and many of her fondest memories in life took place there. Her parents had always dreamed of turning the farm into an affordable family-friendly experience with hayrides, apple picking, and more. Eventually they decided to proceed with the commercialization of the farm, and it worked very well. Too well. They weren't able to keep up with demand without hiring more people, and they couldn't get good talent without offering health benefits. Ashley's parents didn't understand the detailed options of offering benefits. They were sold a benefits plan that wasn't feasible for them in the long run. Due to high healthcare costs, the overall increasing price of talent, and additional business expenses, they were losing money. The situation forced them to make the very hard decision to close the farm. They lost a sizeable source of income. Their only option was to sell the farm. The whole family was devastated.

Ashley became passionate about helping small businesses avoid this kind of life-changing mistake, so she switched career paths and got into the insurance industry. Now she finds a great deal of reward in empowering small business owners through education, teaching them about risk reduction, and offering the right solutions to meet their goals. This story is her Why, and I know from firsthand experience that she cannot tell it without getting emotional.

Example 3 - Ticket Sales: Matt, one of my past clients, was exposed to baseball from a very young age. He spent a lot of time with his grandpa, and instead of sitting around the house, they went to baseball games. To Matt, it wasn't about watching the game as much as it was about hanging out with his grandpa. They had a great time together sitting in the stands. They enjoyed being outside and treating themselves to the stadium's snacks. When Matt's grandpa passed away, Matt would still go to baseball games, but the experience was different. It made him think about how many other people in the stands were having meaningful experiences with loved ones at the ballpark, and that inspired him to work in the baseball industry.

Today, Matt sells tickets for a minor league team, and he is nothing if not passionate about his job. He talks about how each baseball game, although full of excitement, energy, and enthusiasm, could be the very last one for many people in attendance because God may call them home shortly. He works hard to get people into the stands, and to make every game extremely memorable and enjoyable for them. During games, you can find him walking around striking up conversations with strangers and passing out free swag.

Example 4 - Medicare Supplements: Grace went through my Group Cold Call Training Program a few years back, and I remember her distinctly because she had been retired for a few years before deciding to get into sales. (I've helped people in a range of industries, but she was my first retiree-turned cold caller.) After Grace stopped working, she developed a serious health condition. It required surgery, and she was in and out of the hospital for over a year as doctors struggled to properly diagnose her and develop an effective treatment plan. Throughout this time, she was on Medicare, but it didn't cover all of her expenses. By the time she was well enough to get on with her life, she found herself under a crushing amount of debt. She slipped into a deep depression and began to feel like a totally different person. Her husband left her, and her two adult daughters blamed her for the unraveling of their marriage. Both daughters cut her out of their lives.

After a period of reflection and soul-searching, Grace realized she couldn't do anything to get her husband or daughters back, but moving forward, she could help others avoid going through the same kind of financial hardship that created a downward spiral in her life. She decided to get into the Medicare supplements industry. All her work is done over the phone and sharing her Why helps her connect with POIs authentically, showing them that she truly does care and can relate to them in a manner that most people simply cannot.

Exercise - Write down your Why story

It takes time to craft a world-class story around your Why, so give this task the attention it deserves. I promise that it will be worth it! When you can tell an interesting story that explains why you're passionate about your current role, POIs will remember you. You will stand out from the crowd and cut through the noise of your competitors. In sales, this is the majority of the battle.

In the coming chapters, I'll show you how to give POIs a taste of your Why in your personalized cold call script.

5

THE FIVE FUNDAMENTALS OF COLD CALL PSYCHOLOGY

Many sales trainers focus on getting into the right state of mind for cold calling. People hang up on you, they yell at you, and they sometimes say nasty things. There's a lot of rejection in sales. When you regularly encounter those kinds of reactions, you need to mentally prepare!

But I'm not here to focus on mindset. Don't get me wrong—motivation is important, but that's not what this book is about. And more specifically, when we talk about cold call psychology, we're not taking about *your* state of mind; we're talking about *your POI's* state of mind.

As salespeople, we must get POIs to a place where they don't want to hang up on us. Instead, they are glad they took our call, and they are open to the information we're sharing because it piques their curiosity and leaves them wanting more. That's what this chapter is all about.

There are five fundamentals to cold call psychology. If you master these five concepts, cold calling becomes easy. You won't have to psychologically fire yourself up before every single call because you're not going to put POIs into a mental state where they get upset, frustrated, or angry. In this chapter, we will cover the fundamentals, and then I'll show you how to start putting them into action with your new script.

1 - Keep the call short

When you created cold call scripts in the past, did you start with the message you wanted to share, or did you first set a specific length of time and try to fit the message within the confines of your self-imposed timeframe? If you're like most salespeople I've encountered, you came up with what you thought was the right message, and from there, you didn't do much to adjust the "natural" length of the text. It sounds like a good strategy, but the problem is that it almost always makes the script way too long.

The optimal time for a cold call is 20–25 seconds. Does that seem short to you? Your new script will essentially be a micro-monologue. The clock starts when your POI picks up the phone; it ends when you're done with your portion of the message. You don't want to be on cold calls much longer than 25 seconds because the longer you speak, the more likely you are to self-incriminate, i.e., say something that makes POIs believe they are on the receiving end of a sales call. The conversation will go south quickly.

It reminds me of a sign we had hanging in the bathroom when I was growing up. It said: "Welcome! Make yourself comfortable. But remember, how long 10 seconds is depends upon which side of the door you're on." It's so true! When you're making sales calls all afternoon, spending a few minutes talking to someone might seem like a blip on the radar. But when you're not expecting a sales call and it's interrupting whatever you're doing, time goes much slower. People don't like unsolicited calls from individuals trying to get them to buy something. When you keep it short, POIs hardly have time to realize they're on a sales call. That's ideal.

2 - Pique curiosity

I have good news and bad news. Let's start with the bad. I can't tell you specifically what to say to leave your POIs wanting more. I can't do it because everyone is unique. We have different motivations with respect to our self-interest and self-preservation. But don't fear! Instead of telling you exactly what to say to pique curiosity, we'll model your script after something that has been proven to be one of the most effective methods for generating interest: a movie trailer.

Think about it—you're on a date night with your partner. You've already paid a small fortune for the tickets and concessions. Maybe you also have a babysitter you're paying by the hour, so time is money. The movie you're excited to see was supposed to start at 8:30, but before it plays, you're going to be shown 20 minutes of previews. And honestly, you're going to (at least kind of) enjoy it.

It's rare for a person to gladly sit through a lengthy sales pitch. Perhaps even look forward to it. Movie trailers work! They pique customers' curiosity and make the movie industry a ton of money in the process. If we model cold calls off movie trailers, we can craft a more interesting and engaging script.

Here are four ways we can emulate effective movie trailers while cold calling:

- *Don't give a resolution.* What kind of crappy preview would show the ending? It kills the intrigue! And yet, when most people cold call, they routinely give away the ending. Don't do that! The ultimate goal is to sell something to your POI, sure, but you should never lead with that. After all, if you're at a bar and meet someone incredibly attractive, would you simply ask them to marry you? Hardly! You'd go on a date first and see if there's chemistry. The same rings true for cold calling. There should be no mention of selling in the initial dialogue. (I'll dive into this more in a later chapter.)

- *Only show the best parts.* If the trailer showed you the worst parts of the movie, or the entire flick, you'd never go to see it. Your cold call should only focus on two or three of the high notes pertaining to you personally and/or your company professionally. If you tell the POI everything about everything, why would they ever agree to dedicated time with you?

- *Elicit an emotional response.* Through music, imagery, and scene selection, the movie production company gets you to feel what they want you to feel. If it's a horror movie, your pulse quickens. If it's a romance, you feel that lump in the back of your throat. The trailer engages your emotions and sucks you in. You want to do the same thing with your cold calls because people are emotional buyers, not logical buyers. They may not remember what you said, but they'll never forget how they felt when you said it.

- *Introduce the main characters.* Hollywood is great at selling the actors and actresses who star in their productions, even if it's merely a few seconds of them being funny, heroic, or just downright likeable. In your cold calls, the two central characters involved in the plot are you and your organization. And just like people choose to see a motion picture based on the characters, your POIs are likely to do the same based upon how you position the entities that will soon be playing a starring role in the movie of their life.

3 - Create urgency

If piquing curiosity is the peanut butter, creating urgency is the jelly. Without both, you just don't have a sandwich. When you combine the two, you create something irresistible. And in any cold calling situation, creating a sense of urgency is essential or people will string you along for weeks, months or even years.

Think about all the words and phrases individuals use to get people to take action immediately: *act now, limited time, limited supply, new, buy one get one, get a free gift with your purchase,* etc. Take a moment and try to think of others you've experienced.

Which of the aforementioned phrases/strategies (including the list that you just compiled) is the best way to create urgency on a cold call, if any? In my opinion—and I haven't even seen the list you just assembled—none of them will work with any real consistency. Why? Well, what do all these words/phrases have in common? They're all salesy! People don't like receiving unsolicited calls from sales professionals, so why would you try to get them to take action by reminding them that they are on such a call?

There's a much better way to crack this urgency conundrum, and it's a one-word answer: *might.* This word has the power to get people to lean in and want more. (It can be a synonym, like *probably, could, maybe, potentially,* etc.) And like peanut butter to jelly, "might" needs to be combined with something of value.

I'll share an example of how powerful this word can be. (The following is NOT how we cold call; it's just an example of how the word "might" can create urgency within a person on a deep psychological level.)

Think about your favorite sports team. If you don't like sports, think of something else you would *really* like to see—maybe the symphony or a production at your local theater. Now imagine a friend calls you and says, "Hey, Amelia! I might have season tickets for the Michigan State Spartans basketball program for you this coming year."

Are you interested? Absolutely! Who wouldn't be interested in securing season tickets for their favorite sports team or theatrical performance? But are you guaranteed to get those tickets? No. Why not? The person said "might," which inherently also means "might not." On one hand, I "might" have the tickets for you, but on the other hand, I "might not." You know nothing is guaranteed.

If you really want those tickets, what would be going through your head? Would you sit back and think, "Man, I'd sure love those tickets, but I'll leave it up for Paul to decide. If I'm meant to have them, it'll happen." I doubt it! You really want these tickets, after all. My gut tells me you would lean in, grab the proverbial bull by the horns, and attempt to do everything you could to proactively steer this conversation to an outcome that ends with you securing the tickets. Is that not the definition of urgency?

The word "might" has an ancillary benefit, as well. What if the person in question stated that he/she might have season tickets for you, as outlined above, and then simply stopped talking? If you didn't receive any further explanation on the matter, chances are, you'd have some questions:

- What do I have to do to get them?

- What do you need from me?

- What's the next step?

- Why'd you pick me?

- How soon can I get them?

What do all these questions have in common? There is an inherent call to action running through them. You want to know more! You're looking forward, not backward. Instead of regretting picking up the phone, you're looking to the future. That's where you need your POIs to be! Just like pre-heating the oven before you cook something, you need to warm up your POIs before you ask for a commitment. If not, you're asking them to agree to something they're not mentally pre-pared for, and that can be off-putting to a lot of people.

The word "might" is also incredibly powerful because it's not salesy. If you look back at all the words people use to create urgency, standing alone, they are all very salesy terms. On its own, "might" flies so far under the sales radar that it raises no red flags and arouses zero suspicion. And that's why it works!

4 - Make it about the POI

Any sales leader will tell you that cold calls should be about the POI. (Duh!) But there's usually a disconnect between intention and execution. Consider the following sam-ple script:

> Hi Company President, Paul Neuberger with The Cold Call Coach. How are you doing? That's fantastic! Say, I wanted to call you today because I've been working with sales teams like yours all throughout the area and they are putting up some incredibly amazing numbers on the phone as a result. However, a sales team as unique as yours deserves a unique cold calling solution. With that being said, I'd love to learn more about your goals, your challenges, the people on your team, and what you would like to accomplish with a program like this so I could build one customized to meet the needs of ABC Manufacturing. Can I stop by next Tuesday?

Who is this script about—me or the POI? Maybe it's hard to decide. It sounds like I want to help POIs and I'm planning on tailoring my services to meet their needs. But that doesn't necessarily mean the call is about them. Luckily, there's a simple, objective way to tell if the script you're using is about the salesperson or the POI. Ask yourself, "Based upon what I say and how I say it, who benefits first, me or the POI?"

In this case, I would benefit first. I'd meet with the POI, design a customized solution, pitch it to him, and get his business. Then I'd help execute the solution. I benefit first because he pays me, then he benefits by getting what I sold him after I cashed the check. So, the call is about me—not him. If you receive an unsolicited call from an unregistered number from a person you've never heard of from a company that you're not familiar with, and the person on the other end of the line stands to benefit first, what type of call is it? A sales call!

When you focus on crafting a POI-centric script, the call will look and feel very different. Let's go back to the definition of a successful cold call: getting dedicated time. It's not about qualifying, selling, or proactively getting POIs to fall in love with you. Just get on their calendar! With that in mind, consider another script:

> Hi Company President, Paul Neuberger with The Cold Call Coach. How are you doing? That's fantastic! I just wanted to call you today to say thank you. Your organization is doing some truly incredible things and because of all the success you're having, you're improving the local economy and making this a better place to live, work, and play. When the local economy does better, businesses such as mine do better and I am grateful for your efforts. Now it's nothing big,

but the guys on my team and I all pitched in and put together a little gift basket for you. Candy, a gas card, movie tickets—not much. I was hoping to stop by in the ensuing weeks, drop this gift off in person, and shake your hand.

Using the objective test of determining which person benefits first, is this call about me or the POI? It's all about the POI, because based upon what I said and how I said it, Mr./Mrs. Company President clearly stands to benefit first from my offer of a gift basket. If I used this script on 100 company presidents, how many would say, "Uhhh sure... Thank you. You can drop it off to me next week"? I guarantee a much higher number than the previous script! Now, I'm not suggesting that offering gift baskets should be your cold calling strategy, but you can see how different the value is for POIs when they stand to benefit first, not you.

All of my clients cold call to give something—not sell something. This is the ultimate secret to cold call success. What can you give? A resource? An opportunity? A referral? Education? You're only limited by your imagination. If you can tap into the self-interest and self-preservation of the POI, there's no end to the amount of appointments you can secure.

5 - The three worst words of a cold call

There are three words you should never utter on a cold call. If you say these words, it isn't instantaneous death, but you're likely to bleed out rather quickly. The bad news is that you've probably been saying these words your entire career without even knowing it, and it has cost you count-less sales opportunities in the process. Can you guess what the three words are?

My name is...

When a cold caller utters those three words, what are they truly saying? They're saying, "Excuse me, but we've never had the good fortune of meeting, so please kindly afford me the opportunity to introduce myself and tell you a bit more about me." What types of calls usually start out this way? Sales calls! As I've already stated ad nauseam, people detest unsolicited sales calls. You got one sentence out of your mouth and the POI's mood already starts to sour. Instead of listening, the person is regretting picking up the phone, tuning you out, or maybe even actively trying to end the call.

It works much better to greet POIs in a manner that makes them *assume* you know each other. You are not going to lie. I am a Christian man first and foremost and I am morally against lying. Who wants to start a relationship off on a lie? It will come back to bite you at some point. But if you make POIs assume you might have met without mis-leading them by stating that you *have* met at some previous juncture, it's giving you a major competitive advantage. This is a prime example of building a cold call script based upon defense, rather than offense.

I know some of the advice in this chapter is somewhat hypothetical at this point, but that's because I want you to understand the fundamentals before digging in on your new, customized script. In the next chapters, we'll start putting all these elements together to build a script that will absolutely transform the way you think about sales, now and forever.

6

DISCOVERING YOUR VALUE-ADD PROPOSITION (VAP)

The central thesis of my cold-calling methodology is you need to call POIs to *give* them something, not *sell* them something. The Value-Add Proposition (VAP) is where you do just that! In your script, it is arguably the single-most important sentence. It's the hook that compels people to commit to dedicated time with you. In other words, the VAP is the sun and all the other components of the cold call are the planets that rotate around it. I have seen extreme introverts who can hardly string together three sentences in front of strangers crush it on the phone because they have a great VAP. I've also witnessed irresistibly charismatic people struggle because their VAP wasn't tapping into the self-interest of their POIs. Nine times out of ten, the VAP is either the source of cold-calling success or the root of the problem. So, before we get into the nuts and bolts of how to phrase each of the building blocks within your script, we want to start thinking about what we can give to POIs to entice them to take the next step.

As salespeople, we have to remember that human beings are motivated by two things: self-interest and self-preservation. That doesn't mean we are greedy or selfish or materialistic; it's just how we survive and thrive. These motivational factors push us to succeed, not only for ourselves, but also for our families. Keep this in mind as you're thinking about your VAP, and you can tap into your POIs' deepest desires.

When you're calling to give and not sell, the possibilities for offering value are endless, but it helps to have a few guidelines as you brainstorm:

- *You must be able to execute on whatever you are offering.* If you say you might have backstage passes to a concert and currently have no way of getting those passes, you would be lying. Not only would that be dishonest and wrong, but people would be able to sniff it out quickly, and it won't help you close their business in the long run.

- *Originality and creativity are your friends.* I have a number of financial advisory clients who offer a free financial review as their VAP. Is that unique or interesting? No. The offer works sometimes, but they would secure a lot more dedicated time if they came up with something more creative. You want POIs to think, "Gee, I don't get calls like this too often," or "Wow, this is the first time anyone has offered to help me in this way."

- *Your VAP cannot be guaranteed to POIs.* It is conditional on getting dedicated time, since that is your primary goal in cold calling.

- *KISS (Keep It Simple, Stupid!)* Since this part of the script is only one sentence long, you want to go with something direct and easy to understand. We will cover this in greater detail later in the book, but for now, just keep in mind that simplicity is your friend.

The Professional VAP vs. the Personal VAP

There are two different approaches to offering something of value to POIs, and personal vs. professional sounds pretty straightforward, right? Even when salespeople know their options, you would be surprised how often they overlook many of them.

Let's start by explaining the Professional VAP, since it tends to be the easier of the two to understand. Most peoples' first inclination is to brainstorm on how their company can add value. As salespeople, they see their role as being the stewards of this value, simply presenting it to POIs on cold calls.

When you're providing value that is dependent on your current job, you have a Professional VAP. If you were to depart from your organization, you would leave that extra value behind. It's tied to the company, not you as an individual.

There are plenty of ways companies can create an enticing freebie or special opportunity for POIs. And when you're at work, it's logical to lead with the professional version of yourself. But from a philosophical perspective, I am amazed at how God has so richly blessed us with many talents and abilities, and yet most people tend to think the only value they can add is dependent on where they work and what they do.

To illustrate this point, I'll use my beautiful wife, Tanya, as an example. (If you ever meet Tanya, you'll know immediately that I married way up!) She was a working professional but has been a stay-at-home mom for the past several years. It was a major lifestyle change for her, as it is for any parent who leaves a career to stay home with their children. Now that Tanya no longer has a job with a paycheck, can she still bring value to others? Of course! (Some of you may think that I am walking a slippery slope questioning this in the first place, but your resounding answer in the affirmative has only proven my point.)

You don't need a title, a business card, or a paycheck to be able to help others. You just have to know what to do! That's where the Personal VAP comes in. It is independent from where you work. No matter what you sell over the course of your career, a good Personal VAP is evergreen, meaning that you can keep offering the same value to POIs no matter what you sell or where you sell it. (And your script won't need to change much if you ever transition into a new role.)

When I first explain this concept in my workshops, I ask if anyone has ideas for delivering value to POIs on a personal level. This is the point in the session where people usually look at me like I have lobsters crawling out of my ears. Most audiences—huge rooms full of people—can't come up with a single thing they could offer to POIs that isn't tied to their job. If you're feeling the same way, don't worry! This part of the cold call script is a little tricky, since it's probably so different from what you've been doing in the past. But if it ain't hard, it ain't worth doing! And when you master the hard stuff, it gives you a huge competitive advantage over everyone else.

Example VAPs

I'll share some of the strongest VAPs to help get you brainstorming. This list is always evolving. Years ago, I started with a handful of VAP ideas, and my coaching clients have since come up with many more. I'll be the first to say it's hard to think of a truly creative way to offer value to POIs, but it's worth the effort! When you find something that works, it's transformative.

I also want to point out that every organization differs on what they are willing to offer to POIs. Before taking it upon yourself to offer anything of value that's tied to your company, you should first get permission from your leadership team.

The Resources VAP: Most organizations are sitting on plenty of resources that their clients would find valuable. It's just a matter of recognizing what sparks an interest and packaging it properly. Maybe you have access to databases, subscriptions, or other educational offerings that your POIs would be interested in. Perhaps you could create checklists, guides, or free webinars. It might take a little work to start offering this kind of VAP, but you're only limited by your own creativity. It's also important to note that once you develop these resources, the ongoing costs of offering them (including your time!) should be minimal, or even free.

The Professional Services VAP: Can you spend one-on-one time with a POI to offer a customized service? Maybe you can run simple analyses with your software to provide a free financial review or a market analysis. What about a 30-minute consulting call? I've worked with several realtors who offer a free home staging session to convert For Sale by Owner (FSBO) POIs into clients. This VAP costs more time per POI than the Resources VAP, so make sure you have a plan in place for delivering on the value you're promising.

The Referral VAP: This VAP is easily the most popular, and it's my personal favorite. Everyone can give introductions to their network, and it's something that can be valuable in any profession. Brainstorm on your personal and professional connections and whether any of your contacts might be excited to get to know one another.

The Exposure VAP: Can you help promote POIs in some way to help them get in front of a new audience? By mentioning or featuring POIs on social media, a website, or an email newsletter, you are giving them the opportunity to build their brand image and get more customers. This VAP is incredibly flexible depending on the resources at your disposal. As a Professional VAP, you can leverage your company's marketing channels. As a Personal VAP, you can tap into your social network, affiliations, and memberships. Maybe your church has a weekly newsletter featuring local businesses, and you want to help the church secretary fill an open spot, so you pass along your POI's name. A particularly effective way to frame this VAP is through speaking engagements. Many professionals enjoy public speaking, and they consider it an honor, as well as a great way to bring in new leads. Telling POIs you want to see if they would be the right fit for an upcoming speaking engagement can be an extremely effective method of offering value.

The Networking VAP: Sometimes it's easy to see why two people might benefit from getting to know one another. If you're a small business owner, maybe you're interested in getting to know other small business owners in the community. Simply acknowledging the other person's expertise can go a long way on a cold call and make it easy to get dedicated time. Note that this is different from the Referral VAP because you aren't framing the value around POIs, but colleagues.

The Commonalities VAP: You can connect with people quickly when you share something in common. Did you go to the same college as your POI? Do your kids go to the same school? Can you find anything else notable from checking LinkedIn profiles? I once wanted to connect with a CEO from a large organization that we considered a "whale." One of our salespeople had been trying to sell to them for years with no success. I looked up the CEO on LinkedIn, and saw he was on the board of a Christian school. I founded an organization for Christian business executives called C-Suite for Christ (www.csuiteforchrist.com), and I thought he might be interested in coming to one of our monthly gatherings. I messaged him and he responded within two hours that he would love to come. Of course, I had zero plans in discussing business with him at the meeting. But if we started to develop a relationship, my professional role might come up in conversation at some point.

Being a salesperson, it's all about who you know. There's nothing wrong with being strategic about expanding your personal and professional networks. And it's always helpful to foster a support network of those who can offer advice and expertise in your specific area of interest.

The Tangible Goods VAP: Do you have any physical freebies, tchotchkes, or thingamabobs that POIs might appreciate? Books? Coffee mugs? Gift baskets? Or maybe even something of considerable value? One of my clients, an organization specializing in professional audiovisual system integration with 19 locations all across the country, offers extremely innovative solutions for corporate offices. From time to time, things would get dinged up in shipping or slightly damaged in the warehouse. Many times, the damage was minimal, perhaps a small scratch or few pixels out on a new monitor. In those cases, this organization would donate the products. When I started working with their sales team, I learned they had non-profit organizations and schools among their clients, the exact places that could benefit from those donations. Talk about a great fit for a VAP! Ever since, the sales team has called POIs and said how they're always looking for non-profits to support via future technology donations, and how it would be great to see if they are a good fit. The team feels good about knowing their donations are going to organizations that can put them to good use, and many times it leads to long-term clients.

The Samples VAP: This can be tangible or intangible, but the idea is to provide a taste of what your company offers. If you specialize in printing, maybe you could send some artwork for their office that demonstrates your company's high-quality production. You could even customize it by printing your POI's branding on your samples. If you have an online product or subscription, perhaps you could share a free month of access.

The Events/Activities VAP: Can you invite POIs to an upcoming dinner event, golf outing, or take them with you to a private club or party? If your company hosts events or you get access to outings through your work, this can be a great VAP for you. But it can also work well if you belong to a membership organization that plans fun activities.

> There may be a cost for delivering certain VAPs, but there doesn't have to be. If you choose to invest in a new VAP, you can more than make up for it in new business. If you're reading this book on your own instead of with your sales team, I encourage you to approach your sales manager and talk about potential VAPs. Be innovative, creative, and engaged. Taking the initiative to suggest something new is always appreciated by individuals in leadership!

Coming up with a strong VAP does not happen instantly. It just might strike you like a bolt of lightning. But when I work with teams, it typically takes a few sessions to really nail down a good VAP. My best advice is don't settle on your first idea. Get creative, give it time, and don't be afraid to suggest options that seem silly or outlandish! Unique ideas go a long way in catching POIs' attention.

Courting POIs

Now, you may be wondering what happens when POIs take you up on your VAP. They agree to spend dedicated time with you, mostly because they want whatever you offered. Your first interaction should be about them and the VAP—not about you. It's like a date with zero sexual tension! You're not there to go home with the person. You're not trying to sell anything. You are there to get to know them and figure out if they are the right fit for your VAP. More importantly, you are there to get them to like you. People do business with people they like.

You have to court POIs, just like in dating. You can't just approach a person on the street who catches your eye and ask them to marry you. The same holds true in sales. There's a process of getting to know one another that needs to happen first. And in getting to know the other person, you'll gain the intelligence you need to offer value and enhance the relationship.

The reality is that not all VAPs can be executed right away. If you have swag that's sitting around gathering dust or tickets to an event next week, you can fulfill your VAP within days. But after the VAP, you want to keep delivering value, so the relationship doesn't end as quickly as it started. And for VAPs that can't be delivered right away, you need to show you weren't being disingenuous when you made the initial offer. If you said you wanted to consider the POI as a speaker, but your company's conference is 11 months away, you'll want to come up with other options for offering value before then.

A key goal for your first meeting with a new POI should be for you to leave with at least one piece of actionable intelligence. This is one thing you can assist with, aside from the VAP, that goes above and beyond what you are paid to do.

As an example, one woman I coached was meeting with a new POI for the first time, and she noticed he was drinking Orange Mountain Dew. She commented on it, and he said it's his favorite drink, but it can be very hard to find. He mentioned that he likes to stock up on it, and his supply was running low. A few weeks later, the salesperson saw Orange Mountain Dew in a store, so she bought three cases for him. She delivered it to his office a few days later along with a handwritten card thanking him for getting together to chat. A few months later, he become her client. Sometimes the little stuff goes a long way!

It may feel like we're getting a bit ahead of ourselves by talking about what happens when delivering the VAP, but I think it's important for you to understand what's coming. You'll have a better line of sight when it comes to creating a VAP and envisioning what it will be like to execute on it when you get dedicated time. It's also essential to understand how the VAP works to fully comprehend the other elements of the script, since they will all be customized around the VAP. In the next chapter, I'll break down each part of the script so you can see how they all work together.

7

THE BUILDING BLOCKS OF THE COLD CALL SCRIPT

The only thing that is truly consistent in life is change. Companies expand their service offerings and we find ourselves selling new products, or perhaps we transition to a new role and sell something else for the same company. My cold call script methodology is rooted in developing a script that works forever instead of only for a solitary moment in time. Who wants to reinvent the wheel over and over again? No one! Instead of giving you a fish and feeding you for a day, I'm going to teach you how to fish and feed you for a lifetime.

First, we'll break down the script to understand the purpose of every single word you will utter on the phone. I call this process "script diagraming." You may remember those lovely days in high school where you were called up to the front of the room to diagram sentences in English class. By learning all the parts of a sentence, you got an understanding of how to become a better writer. Script diagraming works in much the same way. We'll learn which types of words and phrases to avoid on your cold calls, no matter who you are or what you're selling. Although no two people will end up with the same script, I'll show you how anyone can use these building blocks to create a compelling narrative that works day in and day out.

The script-creation process offers a lot of flexibility in terms of the content, but it follows three basic parameters:

1. Your cold call script must consist of five parts, building blocks, in a certain order.

2. Your cold call script must consist of six sentences. No more, no less. (You may be thinking, "Wow, that's specific!" Yes, it absolutely is! I have this thing down to a science, after all.)

3. Your cold call script must be between 20–25 seconds in duration.

These are the basic rules. If you deviate from this formula, don't come crying to me when you're still struggling on the phone! You simply will not have the same level of success if you don't follow these three rules.

The Five Building Blocks

In the following chapters, I will describe each building block in greater detail, but I want to give you an introduction to all five now so you can see them together and get a better picture of what your script is going to look like as a whole.

1. **The Assumptive Greeting:** You want to greet POIs in an upbeat manner that makes them assume you've met. This gets the call off to a solid

start. That said, the number-one thing I want to convey to you is that you cannot lie on a cold call. Don't be deceptive! However, you don't have to tell POIs everything right up front. In the next chapter, I will show you how to do this with skill and grace.

2. **The Attention Trigger:** People multitask, they have short attention spans, and even when you get them on the phone, a lot of times they aren't really listening to you. But you need their full attention on the cold call, or they might miss the important information you'll share later. The purpose of this part of the script is to win their undivided attention to ensure you get dedicated time.

3. **The Value-Add Proposition (VAP):** As discussed in the previous chapter, this is the portion of the script where rather than calling to sell the POI something, you are calling to give the POI something. It tunes into WIFM, everyone's favorite radio station: *What's In it For Me.* A good VAP will speak to the individual who picks up the phone, rather than the organization overall, since people are primarily concerned with self-interest and self-preservation. Once you deliver the VAP, the pressure is usually off. But it's a mad dash to get to the VAP because every second it takes you to get there, you run the risk of having an unsuccessful call because people usually assume you're selling

something. You need to smack them in the face with overwhelmingly positive value. After that, you can slow down and fill in the blanks.

4. **Establish Credibility:** This is where you connect the dots and tie the script together. Up to this point you haven't really said much. You've said your name, but it's still unclear who you are, where you're calling from, or why you have something to give. This is the section where you fill in these blanks. Chances are, you've been saying some version of this for years, but you've been leading with it when you should have been ending with it. Order matters, and you'll see how putting this part later in the script drives totally different outcomes.

5. **Call to Action (CTA):** If the whole script has worked, which it likely will, POIs will now be wondering what the next step is. That's perfect! This is where you tell the POI that you would like dedicated time. Once you deliver the CTA, you wait for the response, schedule dedicated time, and get off the phone.

The 1+2+3+4+5 building blocks make it incredibly easy to create a world-class cold call script. It's basically a paint-by-numbers activity to craft your own DaVinci masterpiece. With just a paintbrush and a canvas, you would never have known where to put the colors to make a beautiful painting. But when you know exactly where each color should go, it's incredibly simple to complete a work of art.

Before we move forward, I want to point out a very important aspect of making this process work. To get through your entire script and deliver these five building blocks in the right order, you cannot give up control of the call. When POIs start talking, it's a wild card that can hamper our efforts overall. You don't know what they are going to say or ask, and chances are, an appropriate response is not going to follow the 1+2+3+4+5 method.

I ask one question in my cold calls, and it's some version of, "How are ya?" That's it! This question almost always elicits a quick response that allows me to keep pushing forward with the rest of the script. Other than that, I ask POIs nothing.

When POIs start talking, you give up control. You don't know what they are going to say or ask, and that spells trouble for cold calls. I'll show you how to handle objections in a later chapter, but a key goal for your script is to craft it in a way that limits POIs' participation from a speaking perspective.

Sometimes I get pushback from clients when I first teach this methodology. They say, "Wait a minute! We're going to filibuster POIs with a monologue? It doesn't seem very respectful of their time to talk *at* them instead of *with* them." Maybe that would be true if we were saying something boring that they didn't want to hear. Or if we were focused on our own gains during the call. But that's not what we're doing! We're offering profound value, and we're only taking 20–25 seconds of their time. Trust me, it's much better to do all the talking and keep the call under your control.

Now, without further ado, let's dig into each of the building blocks!

8

THE ASSUMPTIVE GREETING

Once people are in our social circles, we tend to respond to them much differently than total strangers. That's why people greet neighbors with a smile and a wave. They typically don't exhibit that same behavior to passengers on a subway train. We feel a need to acknowledge existing relationships and treat them differently than first-time interactions.

As salespeople, we need to leverage this knowledge when we're cold calling and use it to our advantage—without being dishonest or misleading.

I always start out my cold calls with an extra-enthusiastic and personable tone of voice. I sound as excited to speak with POIs as I sound when calling an old friend. With this in mind, I start my calls with something like this:

- *Hey Brian! Paul Neuberger. How've ya been?*

- *Good morning, Mike! Paul Neuberger. What's new?*

- *Hi Vicki! Paul Neuberger. What's been happening?*

The phrasing is important here. "How've ya been?" implies that I used to know how you were. "What's new?" suggests that I know what's old. And "What's been happening?" insinuates that I used to know what was happening. It's subtle, but it's there.

Human beings are complicated creatures, but I know a couple of important things about our species. The first is that we are social animals. Is it possible that Brian has met Paul Neuberger at some point in the past, but is simply not recalling when or where at this exact moment? Maybe he bumped into someone named Paul Neuberger at one of the billion networking events he's been to but can't remember which one. I didn't say anything salesy or self-incriminatory, I have energy and enthusiasm in the greeting, I don't sound like a salesperson after the first sentence, and I don't immediately lose his attention when I introduce myself. It's incredible how well this works! In fact, it's downright comical how often people pick up the phone by saying "Hello?" in a low baritone, then raise their voice to a pitch reminiscent of someone inhaling helium from a balloon after they hear overt friendliness on the other end without a salesy introduction. An elevation of their mood to commence the call, even if only temporary, ensures that we get a running start out of the gate.

The second thing I know about humans is that no one wants to look stupid. When you use a greeting that is assumptive in nature, you've got the POI in a rather awkward spot. We've all been there—when someone seems to know you, and for the life of you, you cannot figure out who they are or how you know them. You try to buy time and not let on that you're confused. You don't want to just ask them who they are because maybe you met them a couple of weeks ago and spent 10 minutes talking about your business. Or maybe they're your sister's friend's cousin's ex-boyfriend. You would look like an idiot and a self-absorbed jerk if you don't remember them, right? To avoid this embarrassment, you try to figure out who they are without making any indication you don't know. This is standard behavior for people across the board, and because we know this is how people respond, we can parlay this to our favor on the cold call.

Without the corresponding visual cues present when meeting in person, POIs must listen hard to collect clues. And when they are hanging on your every word, they aren't trying to get you off the phone. They aren't multitasking. You have their sole, undivided attention. This will typically buy you a 10- to 15-second grace period. And since your scripts will only be 20–25 seconds long, you're almost done with the call by the time they figure out they don't know you.

When I share this strategy in workshops, someone invariably asks, "Won't people be upset when they find out they don't really know you?" For starters, I never said I did know them. I laid it on thick with a friendly, Assumptive Greeting, but by the time they realize we've never met, it doesn't matter because I'm giving them something that taps into their self-interest and they are thrilled that they took my call.

When was the last time you got mad at someone who was overtly friendly, who then offered to help you get something you really wanted? My point exactly.

THE NON-ASSUMPTIVE QUESTION

I've coached thousands of salespeople over the years, and I know that some of them are just flat-out uncomfortable asking a question that makes POIs assume they've met before. No matter how many times I explain that there's nothing inherently wrong with this strategy and that it can truly help the rest of the script go like clockwork, they don't want to do it. And I must respect that. I want my methodology to work for everyone.

It's important to feel confident, comfortable, and natural delivering your script. If you simply cannot imagine uttering an assumptive question to POIs, it's not a deal breaker. You can go without it.

Here are a few examples of non-assumptive questions you can ask POIs:

How is your day going today?

Did you have a nice weekend?

Did you watch the Green Bay Packer game on Sunday?

Ask these questions in an upbeat and overtly friendly tone intended on brightening the POI's day. If you do this well, execute on the rest of the script, and have a high-quality VAP, you can still transform your cold-calling results.

The Assumptive Greeting might take a little practice to get good at it, since it's probably different from how you've been starting your calls previously. Even if you're a little skeptical, I urge you to at least try it. When you only have 20–25 seconds on the phone, nuance matters. Getting out of the gate with a full head of steam makes a huge difference in your calls, and mastering the Assumptive Greeting will put you in a great spot for success with the rest of the script.

9

THE ATTENTION TRIGGER

Out of all five parts of the cold call script, the Attention Trigger is arguably one of the most challenging because it's so different from any strategy that you've previously employed. This part of the script is a one-sentence, fail-safe method of captivating POIs' attention in case the Assumptive Greeting doesn't totally reel them in. Since we go into the VAP right after this, POIs must be completely focused on us and our conversation before we punch them in the face with value.

So, how do we do this? We need to flip the script with a twist that surprises people. It's the same principal that John F. Kennedy followed in his 1961 inaugural address when he said, "Ask not what your country can do for you, but what you can do for your country." This statement surprised the American people and knocked them back on their heels. They didn't expect this brand-new president to ask something of them right then, and it changed people's perspectives. When we use the tactic of flipping the script on cold calls, it throws people off for a moment and gives us more room to maneuver.

Most sales calls convey one of the following:

- This is why you (POI) need me (salesperson)
- This is what I (salesperson) can do for you (POI)

If you can think of every script you've ever heard, they probably all follow one of these formats. I'll say it one more time: people don't like receiving unsolicited sales calls! When your call takes the form of those listed above, POIs will figure out they are suddenly on an unwanted sales call. But when you flip the script, it throws people off and gets their attention by leveraging the element of surprise:

- This is why I (salesperson) need you (POI)
- This is what you (POI) can do for me (salesperson)

You want your Attention Trigger to spark questions in your POIs' minds. When they are engaged and curious, they want to continue the call. They want to know more. This is exactly where you want them to be.

The Attention Trigger is going to flow into your VAP, where you offer something of value that taps into POIs' self-interest and self-preservation. After reading Chapter 7, you might already be mulling over a few potential VAPs, such as referrals, speaking engagements, or bonus resources from your company. When you flip the script, you find a creative way to introduce the unique value you can offer POIs.

Generic vs. Specific Attention Triggers

You have two options for this part of the script—a Generic Attention Trigger or a Specific Attention Trigger. These options allow for further customization so you can create something that feels comfortable and authentic.

Generic Attention Triggers can be used on any person in any call at any time, whether you're calling the president of a global corporation or the garbage man. In other words, it is not related to the POI's role. Here are a few examples:

Hi Amelia, Paul Neuberger. How've ya been?... Great!

- *I'm in need of your assistance.*

- *I wanted your feedback on something real quick.* (Not perfect grammar, but sometimes a more informal approach can work better for you.)

- *I am hoping to tap into your expertise.*

People like to feel valuable to others. While a POI might not be jumping out of their chair with a desire to schedule dedicated time just yet, they aren't seeking to end the call. The element that makes this work is surprise. I could be anybody! And this certainly doesn't sound like a sales call. The person on the other end could be a friend, a friend of a friend, a professional acquaintance, or someone who wants to hire you. You don't hang up yet because you're too intrigued.

Specific Attention Triggers are a little different because they are tied specifically to a POI's role and responsibilities within their company. The information feels personalized, which makes the hook a little stronger. Here are a few examples of Specific Attention Triggers that might work if I was calling an HR Director:

Hi Amelia! Paul Neuberger. How've ya been?... Great!

- *I was hoping to get your feedback on a personnel matter.*

- *I have a personnel matter to put on your radar.* (It doesn't flip the script a ton, but it almost seems like I'm doing the POI a favor.)

- *Your insight on a personnel issue would be greatly appreciated.*

Do you see how these options are more compelling than Generic Attention Triggers? They give POIs a little more meat to sink their teeth into. I always recommend going with a Specific Attention Trigger if you can, but of course, it's dependent on your VAP. I couldn't call a POI with the aforementioned Attention Triggers unless my VAP could actually be related to a personnel issue.

It's important to note, if you develop a Specific Attention Trigger for POIs who are HR Directors, it likely won't work on CEOs, CFOs, VPs of Sales, etc. because they all serve different functions within the organization. If your POIs are concentrated into one role or job function, developing a Specific Attention Trigger can work very well. But if you call POIs in a variety of roles, it becomes a little more complicated.

To develop a compelling Specific Attention Trigger, you must put yourself in your POIs' shoes and ask two questions:

1. What are they accountable for in their specific role within the company?

    For instance, if you call HR Directors, they might handle personnel issues, compliance, employee engagement, and/or recruiting.

2. Who would your POIs like to get a call from?

    I'll give you a hint: the answer is never, ever a salesperson. They do not want an unsolicited call from someone who can save them money or make their life easier with a new service or product. That's a sales call! So even if they would ultimately be happy with a new service or product, they will not be chomping at the bit to take your call.

So, if they don't want to talk to salespeople, who's left? If you think about your POIs' job responsibilities, it'll help you home in on some options. For example, if POIs oversee recruiting, maybe they would like to get a call from an interested job applicant. Or maybe a fellow HR director they can talk shop with. Or maybe they would like to get a call from someone who can tip them off to a potential issue in their organization before it becomes a real problem.

Again, you are not going to lie about who you are. But thinking from this perspective will help you figure out how to craft the perfect sentence that grabs people's attention and helps you properly position your VAP.

Let's go back to the previous examples of calling POIs about a personnel issue. Before I was President of The Starr Group, in my role as Founder & CEO of The Cold Call Coach, I was a consultant for their team of producers, including the individuals who worked in their Group Benefits Department. They were always calling HR Directors. One thing their company offered to new customers was a free review of their employee handbook. They hired an HR consultant, and they covered that cost on their own dime. The Starr Group used to only offer this service to customers, but after discussing the matter further, they started to offer it to POIs as a Professional VAP to get in the door with them. (Why offer value *after* the fact when you can run more appointments with POIs by offering it *before* you do business with them?) So, the sales team started using a version of the Attention Trigger above, and they talked about the free employee handbook review as their VAP. It went something like this:

> *Hi Amelia, Paul Neuberger. How've ya been?... Great! I have a personnel matter to put on your radar. I might be able to offer you a complimentary review of your employee handbook.*

The Specific Attention Trigger engages POIs by talking about something that taps into what they are accountable for—personnel matters. It's just enough information to catch them off-guard and pique their interest. From there, the VAP does the heavy lifting of reeling them in.

As we go through the remaining parts of the script and you gain a better understanding of how everything works in concert, you can come back to this chapter and think more about whether you want to go with a Generic Attention Trigger or a Specific Attention Trigger.

Now, let's dig in and talk about presenting the VAP in your script.

10

THE VAP

Your VAP is the hook that compels people to commit to dedicated time with you. That makes this portion of your script the most important part of your cold call.

By this point in your journey, you should have made good progress in determining the value you might want to offer on your cold calls. Maybe you're already perfectly positioned to start providing value through professional resources, networking, or samples. Or maybe you have a good idea for a VAP, but you need to put in work before you can make it a reality. Now is the time to start doing that! We are more than halfway through this book, and by the time you finish reading, I want you to be ready to start putting the lessons into action. If you need to put in time and effort to create your VAP, get moving!

Some of the greatest VAPs I've ever seen were developed by organizations going through my training program. I worked with a recruiting and staffing firm that wanted their whole team to use the exposure VAP, but they didn't have any strong marketing efforts in place that would appeal to their POIs. They decided to create an "HR Spotlight" feature that would highlight a couple of successful HR directors each month, both on their website and in an email newsletter. They kicked off the new program by including some of their current clients, and then they started leading with it in their cold calls. It worked like a charm!

If you're considering offering a personal VAP rather than a professional VAP tied to your company, chances are you should be doing something right now to make your offer that much stronger in anticipation of your upcoming cold calls. For example, if you choose the referral VAP, you should focus on how to build your network and forge more connections with COIs. If you're interested in the exposure VAP, you should be expanding your online presence, and/ or getting involved in more membership associations and clubs. These kinds of things take time, and quite frankly, should be considered an ongoing project. (I am a member of a few associations just because they have regular meetings and bring in guest speakers. Hello, exposure VAP!)

Since offering value is the cornerstone of this cold call methodology, you should treat your VAP like your baby. You don't create a baby and leave it to fend for itself. You nurture it, protect it, and support it in reaching its full potential. When the baby becomes a truly important part of your life and you give it the effort it deserves, the outcomes will amaze you.

Script

Some people have good VAPs but lousy messages. Not only do you need a good VAP, but you need to properly frame it in order to communicate the opportunity. Scripts can vary depending on what you're offering, but I'll share some basic guidelines for crafting the perfect VAP sentence:

Incorporate "might": This is the part of the script where you put the word "might" into action (or a synonym, such as probably, could, may, maybe, or potentially). You offer something people really want and create urgency around moving forward *now* by making it clear your VAP is not guaranteed.

Keep it short: I've seen some long VAPs, and salespeople tend to struggle more the longer this sentence gets. Be direct and offer something that is easy to understand in one short sentence. Don't get too cutesy or try to provide too many details. Remember that the next part of your script is Part 4, Establish Credibility, where you have two sentences to talk about why you're offering your VAP. The VAP itself usually doesn't need to be more than a few words. In fact, I tell salespeople to pride themselves in using the fewest words possible to communicate their message. This helps you play good defense and avoid self-incrimination.

Be Clear: Just because your message is short doesn't mean it has to be overly vague. People must know how you can help. Otherwise, you're leaving it up to their imagination, which is not helpful for cold calls. This VAP is too vague:

- *I might be able to help with your marketing.*

This leaves the POI with too many questions. *Help how? Do we need this support? Are we already doing this on our own? How much is this help going to cost us?*

Here are much better versions of making this sentence more specific, depending on your VAP:

- *I might be able to promote you on my LinkedIn page.*

- *You may be a great speaker for one of our events.*

- *I might be able to send some referrals your way.*

None of these sentences drill down into specifics, but they still give enough information that POIs instantaneously understand the value of your offer.

When you start using your new cold call script, it's possible that you thought POIs would be head over heels for your offer, but they just aren't responding as you anticipated. Sometimes salespeople immediately think the problem lies in their VAP. Don't give up on your VAP that easily! It's possible that you simply need to present the value differently, so POIs understand what's really in it for them. You may also have to spend more time cultivating your VAP to get it to the level where it's almost impossible for people to turn down. Be patient with yourself and with your POIs! In the beginning, the value will be brand new to you, but as you practice your script, make calls, and work with POIs to execute on your offer, you'll get to know your VAP better and you'll become more comfortable telling people about it. Before you know it, you'll have so many people who appreciate the value you bring to the table, you won't have any doubts when you're making cold calls.

11

ESTABLISH CREDIBILITY

elcome to the fourth component of the cold call script! This is where you tie everything together. Here you'll establish credibility by filling the gaps you have yet to address, answering the questions that have been running through POIs' heads before they ask them, including the name of the organization you work for and the reason for your call.

This part of the script should feel cozy and familiar to you, since it's probably what you've always led with. But with my methodology, we've moved this information to the second half of the conversation, after you offer value, so it no longer comes across as salesy and incriminating. This simple change in order creates a totally different feel to the conversation.

From the onset of the cold call your goal is to get to the VAP as quickly as possible. But in the process of doing that, you omit crucial information. After the VAP, if executed properly, POIs will be clamoring to learn more and discuss next steps, which puts them in the perfect state of mind for sharing a little backstory on your organization and the reason for your call.

This is the only portion of the script that is two sentences instead of just one. From plenty of trial and error, I've learned that you truly do need two full sentences to fill all the gaps, connect the dots, and ensure POIs understand who you are, why you're calling, and most importantly, what's in it for them. If these items are not addressed properly, all the goodwill that we created as a result of the value offering could be undone.

During my time with Thrivent Financial, when I first developed this methodology my script ended after the VAP, which for me, more often than not, was the Referral VAP. I would simply stop talking at this point and wait for the POI to respond. People reacted favorably to what I said and were usually quite interested in what I had to offer, but I kept getting the same handful of questions over and over:

- *This sounds great, but who are you with?*
- *Sounds interesting, but what kind of referrals would you send me?*
- *Do I have to pay you for these referrals?*
- *Why did you pick me for this opportunity?*
- *How did you come across my information?*

I realized I wasn't providing my POIs with enough details, which was hurting my overall chances of success. I was getting them interested, but I wasn't providing enough meat to establish the credibility that I needed to with these individuals. Out of all the questions I received, it seemed like the main thing people wanted to understand was why I was calling them to offer them something at no cost.

Understandably, this seemed a little weird. It's an uncommon experience. Most people cold call to sell you something, not to give you something. After dozens of attempts, I adjusted my approach and put the answers to their questions in my dialogue. This became the Establish Credibility portion of the script.

The first sentence should inform POIs specifically why you are offering them the VAP. The second sentence goes a little deeper and expands upon your Why. In other words, why do you philosophically believe in offering this value? The best way to answer these questions is with belief statements, which usually begin with "I believe" or "We believe." Talking about your beliefs gives people a real taste of who you are, engaging POIs at an emotive level that will make your conversation much more memorable.

The remainder of the second sentence is completely dependent upon the VAP. If you decide to go with a professional VAP, you will use this portion of the script to give *your company's* Why. If you go with a personal VAP, this portion of the sentence will be used to showcase *your* Why. This is how you establish credibility through the context of what you're offering and bring all the parts of your script together.

Know that you'll never be able to get your entire Why into one sentence, and that's fine. All they need is a taste of who you are and what you're all about to decide whether they want to learn more. The hope is that you can pique enough curiosity to entice them to take this to the next step, which is scheduling dedicated time with you.

Since the Establish Credibility section is completely dependent on the VAP, these two sentences can look vastly different from salesperson to salesperson. Whether you offer the possibility of referrals or a free financial review, your motivation for providing those things will be completely different. I can't tell you exactly what to say, but I can provide some examples from a variety of VAPs that my clients and I have used over the years to help provide a better idea of what this might look like in your own script.

Personal VAP
REFERRALS

- VAP - *I might be able to refer some of my clients to you moving forward.*

- Establish Credibility - Sentence 1 (Why are you offering this?) - *Most of my clients are businesses that have a variety of needs, and from time to time they express an interest in X.*

- Establish Credibility - Sentence 2 (Personal Why) - *I believe in life what goes around comes around, and I'm only where I am today thanks to the generosity of others.*

SPEAKER

- VAP - *My Young Professionals Group might be interested in having you speak at a future gathering.*

- Establish Credibility - Sentence 1 (Why are you offering this?) - *You are widely recognized as an industry thought leader in X, and I think the future leaders of Milwaukee could learn a ton from you.*

- Establish Credibility - Sentence 2 (Personal Why) - *I believe that if you're not growing every day, you're dying every day, and I obsess about professional development and preparing myself to touch as many lives as possible.*

Professional VAP
SAMPLES

- VAP - *I might be able to send you a box of our new, innovative security wristbands.*
- Establish Credibility - Sentence 1 (Why are you offering this?) - *Wristbands are a commonly misunderstood and under-utilized item, and many organizations suffer because of it.*
- Establish Credibility - Sentence 2 (Professional Why) - *We believe it is our corporate responsibility at Wristbands Are Us to bring new ideas and innovations to the marketplace rather than requiring that you go and seek them out.*

PROFESSIONAL SERVICES

- VAP - *I might be able to offer you a complimentary financial review.*
- Establish Credibility - Sentence 1 (Why are you offering this?) - *As a busy professional, I know you are running at 10,000 miles per hour and*

> *you're probably not obsessing about your finan-*
> *cial plan as much you would otherwise like.*

- Establish Credibility - Sentence 2 (Professional Why) - *We believe in empowerment through education at Thrivent Financial, and we think you shouldn't have to pay for information that can protect your loved ones.*

At this point in your cold call, you have greeted POIs in a friendly manner that makes them assume they know you, you've gotten their attention, offered something of value at no cost to them, and connected the dots by explaining who you are and why you're calling them. The goal now is to get their buy-in so they say to themselves, "This sounds great! What do we do now?" Accordingly, the next portion of the script is the Call to Action, and that's what we will cover in the following chapter.

12

CALL TO ACTION

The fifth and final building block of the cold call script is the Call to Action (CTA). It is one sentence where your goal is to secure POIs' commitment to spend dedicated time with you. This time can be in person, over the phone, or a virtual session; what's important is gaining POIs' commitment to further the relationship.

A CTA might sound simple and not worth much explanation or analysis, especially after putting in all the hard work to figure out the Attention Trigger and VAP. If you're tempted to skim through this section, don't! We are nearing the end of the cold call script, and the light at the end of the tunnel is getting mighty big, but we aren't finished yet! I've seen plenty of salespeople get to this point and fail to seal the deal. Your ability to execute this portion of the script at a high level tremendously impacts the results. Endings are important! You need to leave a good taste in people's mouths, and this chapter covers how to do just that.

Statements vs. questions

The biggest mistake salespeople make with the CTA is framing it as a question. Here are some examples of this in action:

- Should we get together and talk about this further?
- Would you like to meet for coffee and discuss this in person?
- Does all of this sound good?

These questions sound like nice, polite, respectful ways to interact with POIs. And it feels comfortable to end your script with a question because it's softer than telling them what the next step in the process will be. But this is not how you want to end your script!

After confidently calling POIs, flipping the script, getting their attention, and offering something of value, they should have one burning question on their minds: *What's the next step?* The CTA should provide an answer—not another question.

Thinking back to the idea that your script should be like a movie trailer, how do trailers always end? They tell you when the movie will be released in theaters! They give a date, or at least a ballpark season and year. Think of how goofy it would be if a trailer captivated your attention, left you on the edge of your seat and ended by saying, "Coming... well, when would you like it to come out?" The same holds true for cold calls. You can't leave people wanting more and then give a weak ending that only sparks more questions.

Keep it informal

It is very important that your CTA sounds casual. You want to give POIs the impression that the cold call is no big deal and getting together in person wouldn't be either. This does not mean that you should make your CTA unprofessional. (Probably best to not invite POIs out to Hooters for a round of tequila shots!) But it's absolutely possible to be professional and casual. This is an important distinction, because making the CTA formal can give a salesy vibe that kills your whole script just when you're about to secure the dedicated time that you are seeking. It plants a seed of doubt in POIs' minds: they didn't think they were on a sales call, but now they are questioning that notion and re-evaluating.

Here are a few words to stay away from, as well as the reasoning behind removing these from your cold call vernacular:

- *Meeting* - Do you picture suits and boardrooms? What about signing contracts? Business language comes across as salesy.

- *Appointment* - What situations require appointments? Dentists, doctors, and other obligations that are about as fun as watching paint dry.

- *Conference* - Who wants to be trapped in a stuffy room while someone drones on and on?

- *Lunch and learn* - If a stranger wants to provide you with lunch while they share information with you, what is the primary motivation? Sales!

- *Webinar* - This is the e-version of everything negative above.

- *Seminar* - The is the even more formal version of everything negative above.

Sometimes it helps to think about the CTA as a first date. Would you suggest something boring, businessy, or otherwise unpleasant if you wanted to secure dedicated time with your crush? No! Don't do it on your cold call either.

Here are some phrases that are inherently casual and work well to keep your CTA informal:

- Pop in
- Stop by
- Swing through
- Say hello
- Shake your hand
- Hop on a call
- Grab a chat
- Find time

A lot of these phrases, if taken literally, don't actually make sense. That's a reason why I love them so much. (How does a person "grab" a chat, anyway?) These options have a little more character and are much less formal than what you would expect from a typical sales call, which is precisely why they work so well!

The rule of three

I'll be the first to admit that I can be rather obsessive at times. One of the things I fixate on is the number three. It's not just that I like the number or consider it to be lucky; I think it has true power. For me, once is an anomaly, twice is a coincidence, thrice is a pattern. Three times really is a charm, and this holds true for CTAs.

You should end your cold call script with a single sentence that lists three specific things you would like to do, including restating the VAP. You need to help POIs understand what's next. They've never gotten a call like this before! They don't know what to expect or what your intentions are now that you have them interested. They're looking to *you* to tell them how to move forward from here. Here are some great options for statements using the rule of three:

- It would be great to find some time, get to know you better, and see if you would be a fit for this free service.

- I was hoping I could pop in, take a tour, and see if I'd be comfortable referring my clients to you.

- I would love the opportunity to treat you to a cup of coffee, ask you some questions, and see if we could work together in some capacity.

Do you see how all these statements make it easy to picture what will happen during your dedicated time with the POI? That's the point! It shows you are confident, prepared, have a well thought out plan, and most importantly, you won't waste their most precious commodity: their time.

Your CTA will be a sentence that's on the longer side, and that's a plus for another reason. After you say this sentence, your script is officially over, and you need to stop talking. To be clear, you should not say another word until you get a response from your POI. Anything else you say after this point is unneeded and can easily sound like nervous rambling. Luckily, when your last sentence is a mouthful, you're more likely to stop talking, take a breath, and successfully resist the urge to end with a weak question. With the rule of three, the last sentence feels like a natural stopping point.

When you craft your CTA, you can specifically state the kind of dedicated time you want, whether it's an in-person meeting, a phone call, or a virtual session with the POI. If it's possible to meet in person, I always think that's the best option. You can read visual cues to better understand what POIs are thinking, and face-to-face interaction drives a feeling of deeper connection. For long-distance opportunities, video chat is also a great option. But it's important to point out that when you say you want a certain type of interaction, your POI might not feel the same way. There's always a small risk of turning them off by mentioning an in-person meeting if they prefer phone calls, and vice versa. For that reason, I typically say, "I'd love to find some time" instead of stating something specific. This allows POIs to decide what works best for them and they usually appreciate the freedom to elect how they desire to proceed in this regard.

What's next?

After you finish your CTA, it's your POI's turn to talk. Ideally, you will schedule some form of dedicated time and get off the phone as quickly as possible. Remember that the longer you stay on the line during the initial call, the greater the odds that you will self-incriminate at some point.

Sometimes you will find yourself with a POI who wants to talk right then and there. There are two schools of thought on this. One is to take it. You have an interested POI on the phone who wants to learn more! The obvious response may be to start the get-to-know-you process on the spot and see where it goes.

The other school of thought probably goes against everything you've ever been taught in sales. It sounds something like this: "I would love to chat with you now but unfortunately, I don't have much time. What's your schedule like on Wednesday?" Asking a question like this is fine after you get through the whole cold call script and the POI is engaging you in conversation. You can see how a directive statement would be rude here (e.g., "No, I'm busy. Let's speak next week instead!") Turning down a POI's offer to talk right then is Ballsy with a capital B! But there are a couple of reasons why it could be a good idea—if you are comfortable proceeding in this fashion, of course.

For starters, even when people say they are free to talk right then, you still caught them in the middle of *something*. If they weren't expecting your call, they might be distracted. So if you say you are unable to talk right then, it forces POIs to carve out a few moments for you as an invited guest in their day. By scheduling dedicated time, you can talk to them when they are truly not busy with something else and they are ready to have this conversation with you.

Another important thing to consider are the skeptics on the other end of the phone who still harbor doubts and reservations about you actually trying to sell them something, despite your insistence on providing them with value where they benefit first. Some may think it easier to just get the whole thing over with right then. They urge you to go ahead and keep talking, but they are waiting for the other shoe to drop. If you say you would prefer to discuss this in further detail at a later date, it gives you an advantage. It's the kind of thing that's just crazy enough to actually work because it gets them off your scent.

There isn't one right answer on how to deal with this situation. You have to weigh the risks and rewards for yourself. From my background in financial advising, I know that some people want the return, but they don't want the risk. Unfortunately, you can't have both. So, when POIs want to talk with you further on the cold call, you must do your own risk assessment and figure out what is most comfortable for you.

This brings us to the end of the script diagramming process! Now that you know the building blocks of a world-class cold call script, it's time to truly make it your own. In the next chapter, I'll show you how to put the pieces together to create your own personalized masterpiece.

13

HOW TO CONSTRUCT YOUR SCRIPT

ow that you understand the strategy behind all five parts of the cold call script, creating your own personalized text is as easy as filling in the blanks: 1 + 2 + 3 + 4 + 5. When you have an exact formula on how to conduct your cold calls, the process becomes incredibly simple. You don't have to overthink it every time you pick up the phone because you've already worked out the best possible message. In this chapter, I'll show you how to write out your version now that you know the process of cold call script diagramming.

Let's start with my first tip: vertical alignment. Sometimes salespeople focus so much on the storytelling aspect of their script that they inadvertently deviate from my proven methodology. They end up with a script that doesn't follow all the rules, which means it isn't going to work as well as it should. To safeguard against that, consider each of the five building blocks of the cold call script independently. On the adjacent guide, you will see the five parts of the script running vertically down the page, along with the top priorities for each part. This guide will help you focus on crafting a world-class message for each building block and making sure your script follows all the rules.

As you jot down ideas for your script, it's helpful to have this list in front of you. I created a downloadable version with room for notes, which you can access on my website: https://paulmneuberger.com/scriptdiagramming/

1. The Assumptive Greeting

    •   One sentence followed by one question
    •   The sentence should omit all four aspects of self-incrimination: saying "my name is," your organization's name, your job title, and the reason for your call
    •   The best questions are assumptive in nature

2. The Attention Trigger

    •   One sentence
    •   Flip the script
    •   The POI should be asking themselves, "Who is this?"
    •   For optimal results, Specific Attention Triggers should be used.

3. The VAP

    •   One sentence
    •   Includes the word "might" or one of its synonyms
    •   Gives something where the POI benefits first—not you
    •   For optimal results, Personal VAPs should be used.

4. Establish Credibility

- Two sentences
- First sentence explains why you are offering this VAP today
- The second sentence gives your Why or your organization's Why

5. CTA

- One sentence
- Statement—not a question
- Informal
- Rule of three

Step 1: Fill in your VAP first. This is the central thesis of your script, and parts 2, 4, and 5 are dependent on it! For that reason, you need to start with #3 and go from there. Go back and reread Chapters 6 and 10 if you need a refresher on creating a compelling VAP.

Step 2: Using your VAP as a guide, fill in the remaining numbers one by one. Treat each one as an independent entity rather than worrying about the overall flow or storyline. It's most important to make sure each part of the script follows their respective best practices.

Step 3: Truncate. You only have 20–25 seconds to get through your entire script, and the shorter you can make it, the better. Review what you came up with for each portion of the script and see how you can make it shorter and more efficient. Here's an example:

- Before: "I might be able to offer you a free financial review with one of our world-class consultants."

- After: "I might be able to offer you a free financial review."

Step 4: Work on transitions and flow. Now that you have a solid draft of all five parts of your script, you can focus on the overall storyline. Read through your draft. Does it make sense? Do the various parts transition well from one section to the other? When you put it all together, does it flow harmoniously? The parts that are most likely to have a disconnect if you are not careful are #2 (Attention Trigger) and #3 (VAP). Here are a couple of examples:

#2 - The Attention Trigger: "I wanted to pick your brain real quick."
#3 - The VAP: "I might be able to offer you a free financial review."

Obviously, this doesn't fit from a flow perspective, which might leave the POI confused and less likely to agree to dedicated time with you.
Or

#2 - The Attention Trigger: "I wanted to ask you a quick question."
#3 - The VAP: "I might be able to offer you a free financial review."

The VAP doesn't even allude to a question, so this doesn't work either.

When I was a financial advisor, I used to call top-producing real estate agents. Not only were their clients good POIs, but successful realtors made great money and had plenty of it to invest with me—should they elect to do so. I put a lot of work into a cold call script that got me in front of individuals like this on a regular basis and it ultimately made a good deal of money for my business. I'll share it as a prime example of a powerful script that flows well and follows all of the best practices we covered earlier:

1. The Assumptive Greeting: "Hi John! Paul Neuberger. How've ya been?"

2. The Attention Trigger: "I'm in need of a good realtor."

3. The VAP: "I might have some referrals to send your way."

4. Establish Credibility: "As a financial advisor, many of my clients have goals to buy or sell real estate, but I don't know enough good realtors in the area to refer them to. I obsess about bringing an incredible amount of value to my clients and want to align them with individuals who have the same values as I do."

5. CTA: "I'd love to find some time, learn more about you, and see if you would be a good extension of my business."

Though it sounds effortless, creating this script took a lot of work! I got feedback from colleagues and friends, learned by trial and error, and revised it countless times until hearing the word "no" from my POIs got so infrequent that I could no longer remember the last time it occurred. I wanted every single word to be strategically thought out so its proper placement in the script dramatically enhanced my overall chances of success.

You should think about your script the same way and fill in the blanks in a manner that highlights your intangibles, hits the POI at a deep, emotive level, and ensures that your conversation with them will be memorable.

Want help with your script?

I work with salespeople in a one-on-one capacity on a regular basis providing feedback on their scripts to ensure they completed the process correctly. Sometimes this is the quickest and most effective way to make progress, especially if you're stuck. For more information, go to www.paulmneuberger.com/scripts and I will be happy to review your script and provide some quick advice in the form of a short video.

14

GATEKEEPERS

ow that you have a world-class cold call script, I bet you can't wait to use it on your POIs! All you must do is get the right people on the phone. But the reality is that depending on who your POIs are, gaining access to them can be one of the most difficult aspects of cold calling. If you're in B2C sales, you probably don't get a lot of gatekeepers. However, in B2B sales, you're often calling a company's main line, rather than your POI's direct line or cellphone.

Remember how I promised you that I would teach you how to get in front of who you want, when you want, for whatever reason you want? One reason why I felt so confident making that promise is because of my methodology for handling gatekeepers. No matter who picks up the phone, I'll show you how you can get in front of your POI with remarkable consistency.

Let's start by defining gatekeepers. You might think of secretaries, administrative assistants, or receptionists. Let's make it simpler than that. *A gatekeeper is anyone who answers the phone that is not your POI.* That's it! Whether the person who picks up the phone has been your POI's trusted assistant for 20 years, or you get connected with a random employee who is answering calls while the receptionist is out sick, I will show you how to win these gatekeepers over and get them to become your advocates.

Over the years, I've become good friends with many people who serve as traditional gatekeepers for their companies. Making calls, I've gotten to know a number of them naturally over time, and I'm always interested in their feedback. How do they feel about unsolicited sales calls? How do they know when they're on one? And what could a salesperson possibly say to get them to let down their guard? I've asked these questions and many more over the years, and this research was fundamental in developing my script methodology. You can be confident that everything in this chapter has been tested thousands upon thousands of times across a wide range of roles, job functions, and industries.

The first thing you need to know about gatekeepers is that you should never underestimate their intelligence. You're not going to put the village idiot at the main gate of the fortress! The professionals tasked with answering phones are often some of the smartest in an organization, and they hold an incredible wealth of knowledge about how all kinds of things are done. They are typically well-trained, and a key part of their job is protecting their colleagues' time. In other words, they have highly tuned BS detectors. When they have the slightest hunch that a salesperson is calling, they're going to try to block access to the POI. That is what they are paid to do! For this very simple reason, it's incredibly important not to self-incriminate.

The quickest way to out yourself as a salesperson is to go fishing for information. A lot of salespeople do this without realizing how obvious it truly is to seasoned gatekeepers. If a gatekeeper answers the phone without identifying himself/herself and hears, "Good morning! Who do I have the pleasure of speaking with today?" it's an immediate red flag. Do clients or POIs ask this question? No. They have a reason for calling, and they're not going to waste their time asking for random information. They would say, "I want to talk to someone in sales," or "I'm interested in the X product," or "Transfer me to John Smith, please." When you give off the impression that you have all day to chat and you would love to learn more about the inner workings of an organization, it feels like a sales call because it usually is one.

Instead of fishing for more information that you really don't even need at this point, stick to a script. No matter who picks up the phone, you'll know exactly what to say. And the good news is that you already have most of this work done. As you'll remember, the cold call script is 1 + 2 + 3 + 4 + 5. The gatekeeper script is as follows: 1 / 2 + 3 + 5

1. Assumptive Greeting

/ Ask for your POI

2. Attention Trigger

3. VAP

4. ~~Establish Credibility~~

5. CTA

You'll notice number 4 is missing. Establish Credibility is the most salesy part of the script, and we want to be especially careful not to come across as salesy with gatekeepers.

It also reduces the script by two sentences, and you want to get through this as quickly as possible.

Let's walk through a couple of examples of what this might look like, starting by breaking down the greeting and the backslash. Say you're trying to reach Aaron Smith, the CEO of ABC Manufacturing, so you call their main office:

> *It's a great day at ABC Manufacturing. This is Emma.*
> (This is not Aaron, so you go into your gatekeeper script.)
>
> *Good morning Emma, Paul Neuberger. How've ya been?*

Pretty straightforward, right? But what if your gatekeeper answers the phone differently?

> *ABC Manufacturing. How may I direct your call?*

How would you answer this? Most people would say, "Hi, may I please speak to Aaron?" This is incorrect. Why? The script starts with number 1, your Assumptive Greeting. You can't skip number 1, and you shouldn't feel forced to do so. It might feel awkward at first, but you don't have to give up control and answer their question straightaway. It's better to stick with the script and proceed with the Assumptive Greeting, except without the gatekeeper's name, since you don't have it. Let's try it again:

> *ABC Manufacturing. How may I direct your call?*
>
> *Good morning, Paul Neuberger. How've ya been?*

They didn't give their name and yet it seems as though you know them by the sound of their voice. They will inevitably pause and try to figure out how they know you and what to say next.

After they pick their jaw up off the floor and utter something along the lines of, "Good, you?" it's time for the next part of the script. Since the gatekeeper is not the person you ultimately want to speak with, you need to ask for your POI. There is no magic formula for this. It can be a question or a statement.

Is Aaron Smith available?

I'd like to speak with Aaron Smith.

Can you transfer me to Aaron Smith, please?

The only requirement that I have for this portion of the script is that you use their first and last name. I always get a little pushback on this, but hear me out. If you're calling a large organization, there could be multiple Aarons. If you ask for just the first name, the gatekeeper might ask you which one. Does that mean you're doomed? No. But it's an unforced error. You are lengthening the interaction, and the odds of self-incrimination go up. It also shoots the Assumptive Greeting in the foot. Shouldn't you know there are 15 Aarons at ABC Manufacturing if you're so familiar with the company? This can raise a red flag for gatekeepers. For these reasons, it's best to always use your POI's first and last name.

The Three Gatekeeper Scenarios

After you ask for your POI, you are at the mercy of the gate-keeper. I have tried to change this and think of a way to get past it, but quite frankly, the ball is not in your court at this point. That said, I can tell you what three things will happen next, and what to say when they occur.

OPTION 1: THE TRANSFER OPTION

The gatekeeper says something along the lines of "sure, one second," and immediately transfers you to the POI's direct line. You are now out of the gatekeeper script. If your POI picks up, you go into your cold call script, and if you get their voicemail, you go into the voicemail script, which we cover in detail in the next chapter.

Don't be shocked if you get a lot of transfer options! You didn't fish when you spoke with the gatekeeper, so you didn't sound like a salesperson. Most of the time, people should put you right through to your POI.

OPTION 2: THE OPTION OPTION

Sometimes gatekeepers will give you an opportunity you might not have previously recognized. As an example, they might say something like this: "Aaron is in the field today visiting clients, but I would be happy to give you his voicemail."

What should you do? Most salespeople would accept the offer to leave a voicemail, without even realizing they have other options! At this point, the call is like a choose your own adventure book. You can go with the gatekeeper's suggestion, or you can use this instance as an opportunity to ask another question.

Some salespeople respond with a bad question, like "When will he be back?" That doesn't matter! You have someone on the phone now, so don't go fishing. Other salespeople might say, "I can try him on his cell. Do you happen to have the number?" That's like tongue on a first date. You're coming on too strong, and you're putting the gatekeeper in an awkward position.

The best question you can ask goes like this:

Actually, can I leave a message with you, please?

The worst that can happen is the gatekeeper will say, "No." This happens sometimes and it's OK! People are busy, and the person who answered might not be able to take down a good message for the POI. If so, be polite and proceed with the voicemail option.

But if the gatekeeper is willing and able to take your message, it gives you an additional leg up. First, it's a differentiator because very few people do it. But this method is also genius because it can quickly turn a gatekeeper into your advocate. If you make a good impression on Emma, she will write down your information, and when Aaron comes back into the office, she can hand him a note and say, "Paul wanted me to leave you this message. He seems like a nice guy." This small endorsement turns Aaron into a warm lead. And when he comes back to dozens of voicemails, it's helpful to stand out with a positive word from his assistant!

When gatekeepers agree to take your message, you go through a slightly different version of 2 + 3 + 5 with your script. You'll need to sub out "you" and "your" for your POI's name and/or pronouns. You also turn the Call to Action into a simple request for a call back. Here's an example:

> Gatekeeper: "Sure, I can take your message. Go ahead."

Salesperson:

> "Thank you!" (Don't be a robot! Always remember to be polite.)
> 2 - "I'm in need of Aaron's assistance."
> 3 - "I might be able to send some referrals his way."
> 5 - "But I am hoping he can call me back first."

After you say this, stop talking. No awkward rambling, no clarifying remarks, and no reciting your phone number. Just wait in silence as the person writes down what you said. This is the best possible way to safeguard the accuracy of the message. People talk faster than others can write, and if you proactively give your callback number at the end, gatekeepers will stop writing down the details of what you said in order to make sure they don't miss the phone number. They'll lose their train of thought and won't remember exactly what you were calling about in the first place. Many people will be too embarrassed to make you repeat the whole thing, and they'll pass along an incomplete version of what you said. Sound familiar? You've probably taken some messages like this yourself! While their intentions are good, it isn't going to help you much in terms of getting a call back.

After writing down your message, most gatekeepers will ask for your number before saying goodbye. If they don't ask, just say, "Oh, real quick, let me give you my number just in case." Keep it very casual and remember to end on a friendly, positive note: "Thanks so much, Emma! Make it a great day!"

OPTION 3: THE PITBULL OPTION

Some gatekeepers can be very loyal and protective. They don't want any Tom, Dick, or Sherry getting through to their boss' direct line, and they aren't shy about letting you know. If you have experienced cold-calling anxiety, Pitbull gatekeepers are likely a partial source of your fear. But dealing with them really isn't that bad, especially when you know what to say!

When you encounter these gatekeepers, you can expect them to screen you for more information. This is in direct conflict with your goals of saying as little as possible and getting off the phone as quickly as you can. When a gatekeeper asks you something like, "What is this regarding?" you know you'll need to execute the Pitbull Option, where the strategy is defense, defense, defense. You should be like a turtle retreating into your shell, saying even less than you normally would.

The majority of the time, Pitbulls will ask questions in an order that aligns with your script, so you can use the 2 + 3 + 5 formula as a guide. However, you should be prepared to go off-script to answer whatever questions come up. It's important that you take each question one by one, rather than proactively giving more information. Here's an example:

You: "Is Aaron Smith available?"

Gatekeeper: "What is this regarding?"

You: "I'm in need of his assistance." (Stop talking and wait for a response.)

Gatekeeper: "Can I ask what kind of assistance?"

You: "I might be able to send some referrals his way." (Stop talking and wait for a response.)

It gets harder to give specific advice from here because it depends on your VAP and what gatekeepers ask. However, when you offer something of value, it usually neuters the Pitbull quickly. The best advice is to continue answering questions in one sentence soundbites. Confident people answer only what they were asked, whereas nervous people feel the need to over explain. Here's an example:

Gatekeeper: "Who did you say who are again?"

You: "Paul Neuberger." (Obviously use your own name here, don't say anything other than that, and then wait.)

If it keeps going south and the gatekeeper is crabby or not letting you through to the POI, you can politely say something like this:

I'm picking up a little hesitation on your side. If you don't think Aaron would be interested in my referrals could you recommend someone who would be?

I'm picking up some resistance on your end and that's OK. If ABC Manufacturing doesn't want to be featured in our newsletter, no problem!

I'm sensing some hesitation on your end. If you don't think Aaron is interested in a free review of your employee handbook, I can make a note of that.

Depending on your tone, these examples can come across as rude, snarky, or passive aggressive. That's not what you want. Make sure to deliver this line with a disarmingly friendly tone. This can work very well, and the gatekeeper will usually put you through to the POI. However, sometimes you'll get blocked, and you can simply call back again in a couple of weeks.

Gatekeepers are wild cards when it comes to cold calling, but you can take comfort in knowing that all your calls will go one of these three ways. You can't be good at anything without practice, so it's in your best interest to do some role playing. Pair up with a fellow salesperson or friend and get comfortable responding to all different kinds of greetings and responses that might be thrown at you. If you train yourself for the gatekeeper, you'll get so good at doing the hard stuff that the rest will be a walk in the park.

15

VOICEMAILS

In my experience working with sales professionals across a range of industries, the average callback rate for voicemails is less than 1%. Basically zero. Why is this? Are POIs not listening to their messages? Are they turned off by unsolicited sales calls?

The problem lies in the quality of the message. People today are up to their eyeballs in work, distractions, and notifications interrupting them through a variety of platforms and devices. They need an incredibly compelling reason to return your call, or they are going to hit the delete button and completely forget it.

People are either motivated toward or against things; they either want to have certain things happen, or they want to avoid having other things happen. When most salespeople leave voicemails, they tend to try to motivate POIs toward all of the great things that could happen if they call them back. But it's actually more effective to use a fear of loss tactic where the risk of inaction seems worse than the risk of calling back. Based on what you say and how you say it, a good voicemail should leave POIs thinking, "I can't afford not to call this person back!" There's a trick for doing this and it follows the same methodology as the cold calling and gatekeeper scripts.

Here's the formula: 1 + 2 + 5 + # + ↑)

1 - Assumptive Greeting

2 - Attention Trigger

3 - VAP

4 - Establish Credibility

5 - CTA

- Your phone number

↑ - End on a high note

I want to point out that there isn't a specific length or time limit for leaving a good voicemail, but we will keep it very short based on how we structure it. First, let's talk about what we're not going to include and why.

3 - VAP: Why not share the VAP in your voicemail? Remember, don't share the ending of the movie during the preview, it completely crushes the mystery. POIs will consider whether they want what you're offering, but they won't truly understand the details. This puts them in the position of deciding whether it's worth the extra effort to call you back and learn more. Some people will call back, but most won't.

I used to leave tons of voicemails focused on 1 + 3. I expected callbacks, but they never came. Maybe they thought about calling back but forgot or got too busy. Or maybe they thought I was trying to charge them for the service I was offering (referrals), which was untrue. Whatever the myriad reasons or assumptions, my callback rate was low. When I switched from 1 + 3 to 1 + 2, it was a night and day difference. It made my business explode, and this was a pivotal moment in my ability to create The Cold Call Coach.

~~4 - Establish Credibility:~~ Why not share these details about yourself? One reason is it adds too much length to the script. The best voicemails are brief. People have short attention spans, especially when it comes to checking their messages. The second reason is you are much more likely to self-incriminate. Even when the information is at the end of the script, it can come across more salesy in a recorded message than a cold call.

Now that we're on the same page with what you're not going to say, let's walk through what you should say one by one.

1 - Assumptive Greeting: In the cold call script, you say hello and ask a question. But since there is no one to answer your query, you can leave it out. This keeps #1 short and sweet. Just make sure to use your first and last name so there's no guessing or confusion about who called.

2 - Attention Trigger: Your response rate is almost entirely predicated on your Attention Trigger. And your Attention Trigger is totally dependent on your VAP. This part of your cold call script may work for your voicemail with little to no tweaks, but you need to consider how it will come across when your VAP doesn't directly follow it. You don't want someone to accuse you of calling under false pretenses. Here's an example:

> *I wanted to learn more about the products you sell at ABC Manufacturing.*

If you use this Attention Trigger on external-facing employees, like salespeople, you will get their attention and they will call you back quickly. But if you go into a sales pitch when they return your call, it will feel like a bait and switch. Don't do that! It will lead to a negative situation, and it can give you and your company a bad reputation.

That said, there's some grey area here. You won't lie to people, but you do want to be provocative and pique POIs' interest enough that they actually want to call you back. A great solution for this is to go with a Specific Attention Trigger. Here's an example from a voicemail script I used when I was targeting realtors:

I'm in need of a good realtor in the Milwaukee area.

Who does this sound like I am? Someone who wants to list my house? Maybe. That's what realtors may assume, but I never specifically said anything about wanting to sell a property. When they called me back, I *immediately* went into my VAP (referrals) to squash any assumptions about the initial reason for my call. Using this script, I had a 95% voicemail response rate—usually within the same day. And what matters even more is that people were not upset with me when they learned the reason for my call because my Attention Trigger flowed perfectly into my VAP.

If you get a sense that the Attention Trigger you use in your cold call script could be misleading, confusing, or overly vague in a voicemail when it isn't coupled with your VAP, you should brainstorm alternative options. You want to feel good about your script while also pushing yourself to gain a competitive advantage. Come up with something different that still follows the best practices of flipping the script. Make POIs think, "Who is this?" It will spark a fear of loss if they don't call you back.

5 - CTA: In the cold call script, your goal is to get dedicated time, but in the voicemail script, you just want a call back. For this reason, you'll include a different version of a CTA. Keep it short and sweet, and don't worry whether it's a statement or a question.

Can you call me back?

I'd love to hear from you.

I'll keep an eye out for your call back.

 # (Your phone number): Do not rely on caller ID to capture your phone number. To keep your message as short as possible, go without saying something like, "You can reach me at," or, "My number is." Just give your number.

↑ (End on a high note): The ending of your message is what will stick in their mind the most. Some salespeople treat this like an afterthought, but it could make or break your entire message. I don't care what you say as long as you are deliberate and enthusiastic. The one exception is ending on the word "thanks." It falls off the table with a thud. And if you try to combat that reality by being overly excited when you say it, it sounds awkward. Here are some examples of endings that work:

Thanks, and have a great day!

I can't wait to hear back from you!

Have a great day, and I look forward to speaking with you soon!

Now we can put it all together:

Good morning, Jay. Paul Neuberger. I'm in need of a good realtor in the Milwaukee area. Can you call me? 555-555-5555. Thanks, and have a great day!

What happens when people call you back?

First and foremost, you should anticipate that your callback rate will increase by what could be a shocking amount. I've seen salespeople go from getting 0–1% of their calls returned to more than 40%—in only two weeks! If you leave 50 voicemails a day for five days, you could find yourself fielding 100 callbacks a week—or more! That is a *lot* of callbacks, and the logistics of handling all of them well further solidifies quality over quantity with your cold calls.

It might sound twisted, but sometimes I'd rather get voicemail instead of having the POI pick up when I cold call. When they call me back, I know I've already piqued their curiosity, and we're more than halfway to securing dedicated time.

The trickiest part is often the timing of those callbacks and being ready to launch into my script without notice. When you're in cold-call mode, you're cheery, you have your head in the game. You aren't self-incriminating because you're sticking to your script. Perhaps most importantly, you know who you are calling. But when you leave a lot of voicemails, POIs can start to blend together. Maybe you called three Garys, two Gregs, and a Glenda, and for the life of you, a few hours later you can't remember who works for which company. When people call you back and you don't know who they are, the sense of goodwill you artfully demonstrated on your voicemail goes away. This can easily make promising callbacks go south in a hurry.

It's much easier to remember people when you have fewer calls. You should also use a tracking method to stay organized. If you take calls at work and you have a CRM system, it makes it very easy to know who's calling and when you last called them. When you're on the go, answering calls from a cellphone is harder. I recommend printing out a sheet of your weekly calls, folding it up, and keeping it in your pocket. When you get a call from an unrecognized number, you can get your hand on that sheet so you're ready to go.

You don't want to avoid calls because you have anxiety over remembering which POI is which. One reason people call you back is because your message didn't make it clear who you are. But when they get to your voicemail greeting that gives your name and title, some people will make assumptions: "Oh, it's a financial advisor/realtor/business development specialist. He just wants my business." That isn't the end of the world, but if you pick up before the callback goes to your voicemail, you prevent POIs from making further assumptions.

So now that we're on the same page about staying organized with leads, let's get to the script. When POIs return your message, they will usually mention what you said on the phone:

> *Hi Paul, got your message. Sounds like you need a good realtor?*

Start by thanking them for calling. Then, to transition, I like to repeat what I said on the script for the Attention Trigger. "Like I said in my voicemail, I'm in need of a good realtor." At this point, you're back into the cold call script. Run through the rest of your script just as you would if this was the first time you dialed your POI: 3 + 4 + 5.

When POIs call back, this call is *not* the dedicated time you are seeking. Dedicated time takes two parties; both you and your POI need to have time scheduled on your calendar. That said, if your POI wants to talk right then, you could have a five-minute call to run through some basic questions you may have about their business. This can help you qualify the POIs, but you still want to be careful not to self-incriminate and compromise the opportunity to get scheduled, dedicated time.

Don't overlook the callback experience

One of my clients had a sales team with an excellent VAP. They were getting great results speaking with POIs, but after a few weeks, their voicemail return rate was only 5%. It made no sense why this number wasn't higher. But when I heard the voicemails that sales reps were leaving, I immediately knew why: they were asking people to call them back on a 1-800 number. Does this seem salesy? Just a little bit! Whenever possible, use a regional area code as a callback number instead of a 1-800 line. Ideally, you want to give POIs a direct number, rather than a main line where they will have to dial your extension or talk to a receptionist. Keep your voicemail greeting short and sweet. You'll have POIs leaving you more messages than ever before!

What happens when people don't call you back?

The average callback rate for my clients is just north of 23% after leaving one voicemail. After years of compiling client data, I can tell you this is much higher than the national average, which is less than 1%. However, the reality is that people are very busy. Even if your message caught their attention and they want to speak with you, sometimes they need a gentle reminder.

In terms of the script, because 1 + 2 + 5 + # + ↑ works really well, you don't want to deviate too much in your callback attempts. But at the same time, you need to say something a little different so you don't seem like a robot. It's also essential to elevate the urgency just a touch in every message.

Keep in mind that your actions for following up with POIs need to align with your message. You are offering something of value for free—not trying to sell something. If you're chomping at the bit to give people a free coffee mug, it's going to seem a little suspicious. For that reason, you don't want to come across as overly aggressive, desperate, or like you're trying too hard.

VOICEMAIL #2

If your first message isn't returned within three business days, you should call back. By that point they probably won't call you back unless you make another attempt. If you left a message with the gatekeeper on your first call, maybe your POI never got it. Opt for voicemail next time.

This script is the same as Voicemail #1, with one slight exception. You add the word "still" in the Attention Trigger:

I'm still in need of your assistance.

The word "still" acts like the word "might." It reminds POIs that you already called, they didn't call you back, and there might be a limited timeframe to want to talk to them. This rachets up the urgency a notch.

VOICEMAIL #3

If your second message doesn't get returned within seven business days, you should call a third time, leaving a final (for now) voicemail if your POI doesn't pick up. Since this is the last step you will take with this POI for a while, this is your Hail Mary. I'll leave it up to you whether you want to wait weeks, months, or even years before you call this POI again. Just know that if you leave three messages that go unreturned, there is a reason this person isn't calling you back.

In terms of the script, you should continue including "still" in the Attention Trigger. You also want to add a sentence that lets POIs know that if they don't take action soon, you will need to move on.

I'm still in need of your assistance. This is becoming a time-sensitive matter at this point.

I'm still in need of your assistance. If I don't hear from you by Friday, unfortunately, I will need to consider other options.

I'm still in need of your assistance, but I need to make a decision next week.

Sometimes you'll leave three voicemails and never hear back. Don't sweat it! If they aren't making you a priority, it's telling you something. Even if they were your most ideal client you've ever called, going after other options is better than chasing someone who just isn't that interested in you.

Some foolish salespeople waste enormous amounts of time calling the same leads over and over expecting different results. Being persistent is fine, but you have to draw the line somewhere. If you overdo the follow ups, you will drive people crazy. They will remember how your pushiness made them feel and they will not want to do business with you—ever.

Using the tools in this book, you have a smarter way to cold call. Do you have other COIs you could cultivate? As those relationships blossom, more of your business can start coming from referrals. If you don't have as much flexibility in going after different organizations, use the "Just Get Inside the House" (JGITH) method, described in Chapter 17. If you can't get the CFO's attention, try going through HR, sales, purchasing, or someone else within the company.

With your new script, you won't win them all, but if you practice and follow this methodology, I can guarantee it will be a night and day difference—both with your cold calls and your voicemails.

16

OVERCOMING OBJECTIONS WITH WORLD-CLASS REBUTTALS

Unless you're brand new to the sales profession, you're probably used to getting objections from POIs. Some companies spend a lot of time training their salespeople to combat these kinds of responses, since they encounter them so frequently during cold calls:

I've already got a guy.

I'm too busy to sit down for another sales pitch.

I bet you can't beat the price I'm paying.

When you're calling to offer people something instead of selling them something, like you are with your new script, the dynamic of your conversations is so different that you won't get the same type of resistance. This isn't to say you won't encounter any questions or reluctance to schedule dedicated time, but you won't get a lot of hard nos.

Dealing with this kind of rejection is what makes sales so intimidating. No one wants—or deserves—to be treated disrespectfully when they are simply doing their job. Take comfort knowing that with my cold call methodology, it defies logic for people to lose their temper with you.

Since POIs' reactions will be so different from what you're used to, let's see what an objection looks like when using your new approach. An objection is any need for clarity that forces you off script. Here are some examples:

Wait a minute, who are you again?

I'm sorry, tell me where you're calling from.

Can you repeat that?

What exactly are you selling me?

As you can see, a lot of these objections seem pretty benign—and sometimes the POI honestly did not hear what you said. However, you can get into trouble if you have to ad lib because it's more likely that you will self-incriminate when forced to go off script. In some cases, that's what POIs are pushing for when they ask questions. They are trying to poke holes in what you're saying to expose the soft underbelly of your story. They try to knock you off your game, trip you up, and uncover your true motivation. You see this all the time in politics when people ask hard questions of their elected officials.

In sales, POIs are simply trying to be efficient. They aren't saying no just yet, but they are asking follow-up questions that could lead them to saying no based upon the quality of your response. If the offer isn't ultimately valuable to them, they would rather take 30 seconds to figure that out over the phone rather than over the course of a 30-minute meeting with you. You need to have solid responses to their questions to show that you truly are offering value for free—no strings attached.

There is a three-step process for overcoming objections: Deflect, Back to Center, Keep it General. When you follow this formula, you don't need to rely on wittiness or giant binders full of answers to common concerns. Addressing objections that way is hard, and it doesn't often work very well.

1 - DEFLECT

My philosophy is to take what they give you, grab onto it, and push it away. By grab onto it, I mean to repeat the objection. This shows you heard what they were saying and are paying homage to whatever is on their mind. It also buys you a little bit of time.

> POI: *"What exactly are you selling me?"*

> Salesperson: *"Actually Sir, I'm not selling you anything."*

2 - BACK TO CENTER

POIs are knocking you off message, so you must get back to your central theme, which is the VAP. Go back to it and reinforce it to remind them of the purpose of your call.

> Salesperson: *"Actually Sir, I'm not selling you anything.*

I might have some referrals to send your way."

Depending on the number of questions they ask, you may have to go back to center a few times.

POI: "How'd you get my number?"

Salesperson: "I got your number from a simple Google search, and I think you would be an excellent attorney to profile on my LinkedIn page."

POI: "Who are you with?" (You must answer this question.)

Salesperson: "Well Sir, I'm with The Starr Group, and from time to time our clients need a good attorney to help advise them. To better serve my clients, I am actively extending my network to meet successful attorneys like yourself."

3 - KEEP IT GENERAL

In *Glengarry Glen Ross,* the actor Al Pacino says, "Don't open your mouth unless you know what the shot is." That's such a great line because it's the truth! Unless you are 100% certain that what you are about to say is going to help, don't say it. One of the issues you face when you cold call is you don't know your POIs very well. You don't want to make assumptions about what they want or like, so it's in your best interest to keep your responses as general as possible, instead of going into specifics.

POI: "What kind of referrals?"

Salesperson: "I work with organizations covering a wide range of industries. I'm fairly confident that a few of them would be interested in learning more about you."

Do you see how this kind of general statement is hard to find fault in? If I had called out specific industries, like healthcare or manufacturing, the POI could have easily cut me off and said they don't work with those types of clients.

When to use the Nuclear Option

Your cold call is a rather unique approach, which can be a bit confusing to some of the individuals who receive it. Some POIs may have an objection or two, but simply because they need clarification. Much of the time, it should be smooth sailing. That said, you need to recognize when you're getting too much pushback and when to pull the plug accordingly.

Confident people understand the value in what they are offering. If someone doesn't want it, a confident person isn't going to aggressively fight it. Pushing too hard creates a disconnect with the script. (Why would someone be practically foaming at the mouth to feature you on their LinkedIn page if there wasn't some type of catch?) Because you're changing the cold calling paradigm, you must change your behavior. You're not going to beg or chase anymore!

When dealing with gatekeepers, we discussed the Pitbull Option and knowing when to voluntarily end the call if you get too much resistance. The same school of thought holds true for POIs.

When I first developed my new script that featured the referral VAP, I was setting appointments left and right. It seemed I was getting yeses all day! Things were going great until a top-producing realtor in Wisconsin hit me with a bunch of questions, one after the other. I did my best to answer each of them, but they just kept coming:

What kinds of referrals?

How long have you been doing this?

Tell me about your high net worth clients.

How many referrals would I get?

What makes you think that I would be the best realtor for them?

Finally, I got so frustrated that I responded in a somewhat rude tone, asking if she could give me a name of another realtor who would want my business instead. The call went silent for a moment, as she was clearly taken aback. I mentally prepared for her to hang up or give me a piece of her mind for snapping at her—which was probably well deserved! But she surprised me by saying, "I'm sorry, who are you again?" I did the whole script a second time, and she said, "OK, I guess we can have coffee." That was five years ago and we're still friends today! I let my emotions get the best of me, I stumbled through my responses, and I'm fortunate it worked out. Most importantly, I realized what I did well: I let go of the opportunity. That's what did it for me; I stopped pushing to try to win her over, and in doing so, I gained her trust.

I learned a valuable lesson about not being too pushy, but I realized I should have backed down a little sooner. After three objections, you start to feel like you are begging, so you need to make the call go nuclear, suddenly giving the POI permission to end the call. You should already be familiar with this approach from the gatekeeper chapter, but here's an example of how to do this with your POI:

> *I'm picking up some hesitation on your side which is totally fine. If you're not interested in these free tickets to my seminar, would you be able to recommend another leader in your industry who might?*

If they say yes, then take that introduction. If they say no, thank them for their time and say goodbye. It's as simple as that! Just like we talked about in the voicemail chapter, if someone isn't interested right now, it doesn't have to be goodbye forever—especially if the account could be one of your whales. Put the lead on a hold list and check back at some point down the road.

With your new script, handling objections should become a much smaller portion of your cold call experience than they have been in the past. But that doesn't mean you shouldn't prepare to deflect, go back to center, and keep your answers general—no matter what POIs say to you. Practice this through role playing with your colleagues. The more you practice, the more comfortable you will be when you get a little resistance on real cold calls.

17

THE "JUST GET INSIDE THE HOUSE" THEORY OF COLD CALLING

Even with the best script in the world, it won't work all of the time. Fortunately, for B2B sales, my methodology takes this into account. Remember how I told you at the beginning of this book that I would teach you how to get in front of who you want, when you want, for whatever reason you want? My "Just Get Inside the House" (JGITH) theory of cold calling is a key part of unleashing this power.

Imagine that a family is enjoying a lazy Sunday afternoon at home. They're sitting on the couch watching TV, when the dad looks out the window and sees a bunch of people approaching the house. They look menacing. Think something out of *The Purge*. They want to reach the family, and if they get in, it won't be pretty.

The mob rushes the front door! Mom jumps up and locks the deadbolt just in time, while dad pushes the couch across the room to barricade it shut. In seconds, dozens of people crowd the porch, pushing, shoving, scratching. It's secure... for now. As the family breathes a sigh of relief, they hear a soft click and the creak of the side door opening. Someone is inside!

I tell this story not to terrify or make a point about the importance of home security, but rather to highlight the concept of points of entry when cold calling. When trying to get inside a house, most people use the front door. Salespeople use the "front door" by targeting decision-makers in an organization; it's the logical point of entry. But it's also the way everyone else is trying to get inside. Oftentimes, they don't even consider the possibility of using a side door or a window, such as calling individuals who are not the decision maker.

Does it sound counterintuitive to contact people you can't sell to? That's a key reason it works! It's time to think differently about who to connect with in an organization. Now that you understand the power of VAPs, you can offer something of value to virtually anyone, enabling you to get inside any organization. Here are five benefits of using the JGITH method:

- **Become a known commodity in the organization:** Let's say you're targeting ABC Manufacturing, and no one there has ever heard of you or your company. It's a cold lead. But not after you connect with Mary from the sales department. She becomes someone within the organization who knows who you are, what you do, and the services you provide. This is a small but important step forward. Mary doesn't even have to like you yet for this to work in your favor.

- **Build rapport with someone inside the organization:** As you get to know Mary, you begin to build a personal relationship. Maybe she will even start to like and trust you, and ABC Manufacturing will become a warmer lead.

- **Rapport can turn into advocacy:** When ABC Manufacturing is considering new vendors, Mary might let her colleague know that they should include your firm on the RFP list, since you've been very nice and helpful to her.

- **Gain incredible intel:** A great thing about JGITH is that you aren't a threat to people you can't sell to, and they are much more likely to open up and share information with you. When people let their guard down, the information starts flowing! As you talk with Mary, she might happen to mention certain pain points or goals they have at ABC Manufacturing, which helps you better understand how you could serve their organization.

- **Offer something of value based upon the intel you gathered:** It's all about value, even when you JGITH. For example, if Mary told you she was having troubling filling a couple positions on her team, you could offer to help in several ways. You could share the job posting on LinkedIn, refer her to a recruiter you know, and/or personally email the job description to some of your friends in sales. Going above and beyond to provide the right kind of help is not only a nice thing to do, it's a surefire way to build relationships.

At this point, all these benefits probably make sense, but you might be wondering what the heck to say to people when you JGITH. After all, you worked very hard to create your VAP for your POIs. Now I'm asking you to connect with other leaders that have seemingly nothing to do with what you're selling.

Remember, people buy people! All you need to do is get dedicated time with a person of influence within the company and offer something of value. Once you get your foot in the door, things take off on their own.

The easiest way to JGITH is to consider networking as one of the most important aspects of your job. Every single day take action to expand your personal network and/or deepen existing relationships. As President of The Starr Group, I have plenty of opportunities to work with my team and help them JGITH. I know exactly which organizations we would love to work with, and I'm always on the lookout for opportunities to connect with the leaders who work there.

For instance, large landscaping companies are great clients for us because they have a lot of insurance needs. One of my producers mentioned a specific landscaper in a meeting, and I filed away the company name in my brain. Soon after, I saw they won a prestigious award. For B2B sales, awards classify as life events, so I wanted to call and congratulate them. I'm also continuously focused on providing value to The Starr Group's clients, and I thought some of them might be in the market for a landscaper.

CFOs are usually our POIs for commercial insurance, but it didn't make sense to call the CFO and use the referral VAP. (He's the bean counter; why would he care about meeting with POIs?) Anyone who isn't the CFO would be considered a JGITH option, and I thought the CEO was my best choice in this situation since we're both the leaders of our respective organizations. So, I called the CEO and left a voicemail congratulating him on winning the award and saying how the timing was perfect because I had been looking for a landscaping company to potentially refer business to. He didn't call me back, but the VP of Sales did. He wanted to chat, so I brought the producer who first mentioned this organization to me, and the three of us sat down in person a short time later.

A well-run JGITH is magical! You can feel the connection from the very beginning, which is how this meeting went. My producer and I really hit it off with the VP of Sales. The whole meeting, we asked nothing but questions about his business to determine whether they would be a good fit for our clients' landscaping needs. (How much business do you do? What kinds of projects? How much revenue do you do annually? Can you describe your ideal customer?) As it turned out, the VP had been trying to get in touch with a business owner who just happened to be a close friend of mine. I offered to make the introduction on his behalf right away.

At the end of the meeting, the VP of Sales finally said, "Enough about me! Tell me what you guys do." I let my producer take the lead on this, and he did a great job describing our company and the services we provide. Part of our elevator pitch touches on the fact that for every piece of new business we bring in, we donate a portion of our revenue to charity. This fact resonated with the VP of Sales, and upon the conclusion of our time together he told us he was "smitten" with The Starr Group.

We never once asked about their insurance needs, but the VP of Sales told us that he would tell the CEO to include us in their next RFP. After that meeting, my friend ended up hiring the landscaping company for a job, and we also referred two Starr Group clients to them. By proactively providing that much value, and continuing to keep in touch, we have a strong chance of becoming their insurance provider of choice when their current policies renew.

This might seem like a lot to invest in a lead without knowing whether it will ever pan out, but it's worth the effort for relational selling. When salespeople and entrepreneurs are successful, people usually just see the tip of the iceberg, the huge clients and impressive pieces of business they write. They make it look easy, but you don't see what's going on under the surface. It might have taken months to make a meaningful connection with someone at those organizations, gain their trust, provide value, and finally win their business.

Sales can seem straightforward, but there is an incredible amount of strategy that goes into doing it well. It's like a gigantic game of billiards. You shouldn't be thinking about your current shot, you should be thinking three shots ahead. JGITH is one of the more complex aspects of sales strategy, but it always comes back to providing value and expanding your network.

It's also important to point out that JGITH can be used as your first attempt to connect with an organization, or a backup plan if you can't connect with your POI. Instead of leaving three voicemails and marking a lead as dead (for now), you can JGITH your way into any organization through multiple channels, anytime you want. This opens up possibilities, which is helpful to remember if you struggle with call reluctance or phone phobia. JGITH makes it so you always have unlimited opportunities for success on a cold call.

My clients have had an incredible amount of success securing dedicated time via the JGITH method, and you can as well. The best people to target are the highest-ranking people in each department, since they probably have the closest relationships with the decision maker. Externally focused departments tend to be the best points of contact, such as sales, community service, recruiting, and even marketing. Refer to the list of VAPs in Chapter 6 to figure out how you can offer value and start helping people. More often than not, you'll ultimately find yourself faced with the all-time best question you can be asked as a sales professional: "Now that you've helped me, what can I do for you?" Now you have the keys to the kingdom! You can ask for an introduction to the decision maker, offer to do a free workshop for their team, or anything else you can think of that would bring you a step closer to getting dedicated time with the person who has the power to hire you.

Just so we're clear, JGITH is not meant to be a manipulative, crafty, or deceitful means to an end. As a salesperson, you make a living from connections. There's absolutely nothing wrong with expanding your network, especially if you are interested in genuinely helping others. Doing so strategically can give you the extra advantage of not only bringing value to others, but getting something in return for your efforts as well.

18

KEEP YOUR HEAD IN THE GAME

Getting your foot in the door is by far the hardest aspect of sales. With the skills you've been learning in this book, you can get in front of who you want, when you want, for whatever reason you want. What could possibly hold you back?

We haven't talked a lot about the mental and emotional aspects of cold calling because once you get going with my methodology, everything tends to become so much easier than what you've experienced before. You won't need to psyche yourself up before making calls. If you had phone phobia or anxiety, it often becomes a thing of the past. But like honing any new skill, there's a learning curve.

The salespeople I train usually find success quickly, but it likely won't be instantaneous, and it won't come without hard work. That means your work is not finished when you complete this chapter. You have to keep pushing! Here are four ways to keep your head in the game and stay focused on reaching your goals.

1 - "TOO BUSY" ACTUALLY MEANS "NOT A PRIORITY"

I'm sure you've spoken with POIs who say they're interested in your product or service, but they're just too busy to move forward with anything right now. When you check back weeks or months later, it's the same story. The reality is that "too busy" actually means "not a priority." The same thing happens when you're too busy to try something new. You're not a victim. You're not a slave to your calendar. You prioritize what's most important in your life.

If you're reading this book, you care about your professional development. Maybe you want to gain financial security for yourself and your family, kickstart your performance at work, or become the best possible version of yourself. As this book comes to a close, you're ready as ever to start making real changes. After preparing, learning, and practicing, you need to take action to move forward. That starts with shifting your mindset and understanding that *you* are in control of your life. Even when life throws you curveballs, you are in control of how you respond.

It can be difficult to carve out time for self-improvement, learning, and reflection, but it's certainly not impossible. Realizing that you have the power to prioritize what's most important to you is the first step in changing your life.

2 - DISCIPLINE DETERMINES SUCCESS, NOT DESIRE

When I was an associate at Thrivent Financial and my boss first asked me to teach the other salespeople in the Regional Financial Office how I had become so successful, I didn't want to do it. I felt like I would be helping my competition, which didn't seem like a smart move. I got some heat for not being a team player, and he told me something that really stuck. He said that even if I shared all my strategies, tips, and secrets with the team, although everyone would learn what to do, very few would actually do it. This was mind-boggling to me! How could people learn exactly what to do to reach their goals, but fail to do it?

Success is a result of discipline, not desire. You can want and wish for things every day of your life, but if you don't put in the hard work to get them, nothing will change.

I meet a lot of salespeople who want to kickstart their careers, but they just don't get around to making their calls. Or life gets in the way and they don't put in any time practicing and honing their skills. I understand. It isn't always easy to create a good VAP, target the right COIs, and spend time cultivating relationships, but these are the kinds of actions that will transform your business. Thinking about doing these things and wanting to do them is not enough. Now is the time to really get disciplined!

3 - DON'T COMPETE WITH OTHERS, COMPETE WITH YOURSELF

I was a skinny kid growing up and felt self-conscious about it. In high school I felt that girls liked the guys who had bulging biceps. Mine were non-existent. One day, I decided to go to the gym to start building muscle mass. I signed up for a membership at Bally's Total Fitness, and during my very first workout, I encountered a man who looked just like the Incredible Hulk! Awestruck, I could hardly take my eyes off him as he lifted insane amounts of weight.

I left that day and I didn't go back to the gym for months because I felt like I couldn't compete. What was the point of trying to get stronger when I was so far behind people like him? All my motivation was squashed in one brief workout.

Instead of pushing to get just a little bit better, I threw in the towel because small improvements didn't seem good enough. The task was simply too hard.

It took me a long time to realize that everyone in life is running their own race, and it's impossible to do an apples-to-apples comparison with someone who is in a different lane. Comparing myself to the bodybuilder at the gym was pointless. I wasn't trying to build award-winning biceps to flex on stage. I just wanted to be a stronger version of myself. A few months later, I got my head in the game and went back to the gym. I focused on myself instead of others, and sure enough, I got bigger and stronger.

As you work on enhancing your cold calling skills and boosting your sales numbers, don't worry about what others do. They have different strengths, backgrounds, and experiences. At the end of the day, ask yourself if you are better right now than when you got out of bed in the morning. If you go zero for 10 with voicemail returns, it's OK. When you get that first call back, celebrate it! Over time, inches become feet, feet become yards, and soon you are lightyears ahead of where you were. Focus on pushing for small improvements every single day in an effort to grow individually and stop comparing yourself to others.

4 - FAILURE IS AN OPTION

People say failure isn't an option, which sounds passionate and inspiring, but it isn't reality. The truth is that all of us fail at all kinds of things throughout our lives. How would we learn and grow if we didn't fail? If nothing bad ever happened to us, we would lose our ability to survive in the real world.

If things don't work out immediately, don't give up! As a sales trainer, I worry most about my clients who start crushing it instantaneously. Right out of the gate, they close huge deals and get lots of attention. Don't get me wrong— I'm happy and I celebrate with them. But it's a lot of success very quickly. Like high school basketball players who went straight to the NBA, they often lack the fundamentals and can struggle with the pressures of their newfound success.

It takes some time and effort to build your skills. This cold call methodology is no different. Your results might not be instantaneous, and if you quit before you give yourself a real chance, you will undoubtably fail. Or you might do well for the first month and then go through a couple of weeks where you struggle to set any appointments. No one is successful all the time. (Even me, and I invented this methodology!) But if you stick with the program, apply yourself, and practice, you'll see real results.

Need More Support?

I've done my best to include the most important parts of my methodology in this book, but it's a slimmed-down version of my full program. If you feel like you're ready to hit the ground running, that's great! But if you feel like you need a little more support, I'm here for you! Here's an overview of all the ways you and I can continue on this journey together:

TEAMS:

- **Customized Group Training Sessions:** I work with leading organizations all over the world to help them bridge the gap between where they are now to where they want to be. Programs are typically 12 hours, and we dig deeper into the content in this book. Group Training Sessions are historically where I've seen the greatest transformations across organizations. To learn more, go to https://coldcallcoach.net/group-coaching/.

- **Keynotes for Sales and Leadership Teams:** I speak on a variety of topics all over the world for both large and small audiences. Get more information at https://paulmneuberger.com/.

INDIVIDUALS:

- **One-On-One Cold Call Training:** I can work with you individually over video chat to provide customized coaching. We would meet for a total of six hours over the course of three sessions, homing in on your trouble spots and refining your script. To learn more, visit https://coldcallcoach.net/individualized-coaching/.

- **Script Review:** Want some quick feedback on your script? Send it to me and I'll reply with a short video telling you why it blew me away, or a couple of changes you might want to consider. Go to www.paulmneuberger.com/scripts.

- **Cold Call University:** If you're newer to sales, this nine-hour program is great for covering all the fundamentals:

https://coldcallcoach.net/selling.

- **Cold Calling for Success Training System:** If you're more experienced with sales, this eight-hour video training package focuses heavily on scripting, hashing out the details that will help you discover exactly what to say on your calls and why.
Visit https://coldcallcoach.net/trainingsystem.

- **The Cold Call Coach YouTube Channel:** Want a free resource with quality content? My YouTube channel features lessons from Cold Call University.
Go to http://youtube.com/c/TheColdCallCoach.

YOUR TRANSFORMATION HAS ALREADY STARTED

My passion for training is refueled whenever I witness the incredible impact of this program on a person's life. There's no sugar-coating that cold calling can be challenging. But since so many shy away from it or do it poorly, a greater opportunity exists for those willing to put in the work.

I got a thank-you card in the mail recently, and it reminded me exactly how impactful this training can be. When I started working with Jason, he was overcome with phone phobia. He was so worried about how POIs would react to him that he could barely bring himself to pick up the phone. To make matters worse, his fear of cold calling spiraled into an even greater fear of not being able to provide for himself and his family. Instead of sitting at his desk, he found himself huddled under it crying. Jason and I worked together to transform his approach to cold calling, create a new script, and give him the fresh start he needed.

Roughly a year after the completion of our work together, he sent me a card:

> *I want to thank you for all of the time you spent coaching and training me last year. The time we shared was invaluable. I can hardly recognize the man and professional I have become. In the past six months I've set over 100 first appointments, opened 20 new accounts and have been asked by the CEO to share my prospecting strategy. I'm in the top 3 in production and I am focused on ending the year as the top agent in the company. I've come a long way from that scared kid crying on the floor to the top cold caller in the business. Thank you!!!*

If you struggled with cold calling, or sales in general, in the past, this is your fresh start, a totally different approach to this modality. You know how to identify ideal clients and introduce yourself to COIs in positions beneficial to you professionally and personally. You understand how to leverage sales psychology to connect with POIs quickly, while driving memorable conversations that show your value. You are well on your way to mastering the art and science behind cold calling—once and for all!

I'm proud to help people transform their cold calling skills, but it's even more meaningful to me that this program goes beyond talking on the phone. My methodology is based on human nature and psychology. It transcends communication mediums. In any situation where you need to influence people and win them over, you use the skills from this book. If you can differentiate yourself, be memorable, and spark urgency in a 20-second phone call, you can do that when you meet someone at a networking event, write a follow-up email, or interview for a new job. The impact this methodology can have on your life is only limited by the effort you put in.

KEEP IN TOUCH!

In closing, I would love to hear from you directly on how this book has impacted you. Please connect with me on LinkedIn at www.linkedin.com/in/paulneuberger! Send me a message or an email at paul@paulmneuberger.com and tell me how your new script is working. If you got over your phone anxiety, I want to know! If you're finally turning gatekeepers into advocates on your behalf, meeting with more POIs, or closing more business, please tell me!

On the flip side, if you're encountering challenges or need more help, I want to know that too. I frequently publish videos and articles that address the questions I get from sales professionals like you. I'm always open to feedback, and I'm dedicated to refining my program to better help others.

Thank you for blessing me with the opportunity to partake in this journey with you. It's a truly sacred responsibility that I don't take for granted. Please connect with me online so we can stay in touch and celebrate your upcoming successes together!

ACKNOWLEDGEMENTS

An endeavor of this magnitude is not possible without the Herculean efforts of many people, and without this team of top-notch professionals surrounding me, my dream would never have come to fruition. I will be eternally grateful for all that these individuals did to help make this happen.

For starters, my COO, mentor, and confidant, Gary Loop, kept me on an even keel during this entire process. His visionary leadership, strategic thinking, listening ear, and tender heart ensured that not only was the project on track, but that I was of sound mind and spirit, especially on the days when I felt overwhelmed by the enormity of life. Where would my life be without you, brother?

I also would be remiss if I did not acknowledge the best business decision I ever made: working with Amelia Forczak, founder of Pithy Wordsmithery. My ghostwriter, go-to marketing whiz, and friend, I could not imagine embarking on another project like this without her. She was calm under pressure, always had a plethora of great ideas, and was able to take my rambling stream of consciousness and turn it into something beautiful. That is no easy task, especially given how fast I talk and how many ideas I have in my head at any one time.

To round out Team Paul M. Neuberger, I also want to thank Jim "Skip" Reinke of Paragon Marketing Group, who shot all of my videos and handled my website work, and Rick Moon of Lunar Communications, who oversaw my blog posts and advised me on my social media efforts. These two humble, driven, incredibly creative men were the force behind my public marketing campaigns. Without them, we never would have created so much attention and exposure for the book. It is a blessing to know you both.

I would also like to thank Jessika Savage for her creative, outside-the-box efforts with respect to the look and feel of this book. As the designer of the front and back covers, she was responsible for the initial first impression, and I believe she hit it out of the park.

I owe a tremendous debt of gratitude to Anthony Iannarino, Wayne Breitbarth, and Jeff Koser, all business luminaries who are changing the world through their keynote speeches, books, and coaching services. They were the first three to put their name and credibility on the line by endorsing this project, and for that, I will be forever thankful.

Finally, I would like to thank the tens of thousands of people who follow me on social media and have supported my efforts over the years. Since the inception of my first business, The Cold Call Coach, in April 2015, I have felt your love, encouragement, and prayers as we have grown into an international organization. Without you, there is no book. Without you, there is no Cold Call Coach.

Without you, there is no Paul M. Neuberger.

ENDNOTES

1   Miranda Brookins, "Success Rate of Cold Calling," *Chron*, accessed
May 5, 2020, https://smallbusiness.chron.com/success-rate-cold-
calling-10031.html.

2   The data was collected by Paul Neuberger from the Town Bank, a
Wintrust Bank team that went through the training program. Each
day for two weeks, the entire team filled out a Call Log with the
results of their efforts.

3   *Simon Sinek, Start with Why: How Great Leaders Inspire Everyone to
Take Action (Portfolio, 2009).*

Made in the USA
Monee, IL
15 June 2020